CASTLES

R J UNSTEAD

A & C Black Ltd

London

Black's Junior Reference Books
General editor: R J Unstead

ISBN 0 7136 0987 7

Published by A & C Black Ltd
4, 5 & 6 Soho Square London W1V 6AD

Printed in Great Britain by
Sir Joseph Causton & Sons Ltd, London and Eastleigh

Contents

Maiden Castle

Acknowledgements

The publishers are grateful for permission to reproduce prints and photographs as follows:

Aerofilms Ltd, pages 1, 4, 6, 10, 16 (both photographs), 24, 26, 39, 40, 49, 51, 53, 54, 62, 65, 69 (top), 71, 74, 75, 77, 81, 84
Trustees of the British Museum, pages i, 13, 19, 31, 35, 52 (foot), 63
Crown copyright, reproduced by permission of the Ministry of Public Building and Works (London), pages 7, 11, 14, 17, 20, 21, 22 (left), 23, 28, 36, 37, 41, 52, 55, 56, 57, 58, 59, 61, 80, 83 (both photographs), 85, 88, 89 (both photographs), 90
Crown copyright, reproduced by permission of the Ministry of Public Building and Works (Edinburgh), pages 29, 68, 69 (lower)
Crown copyright, National Monuments Record, pages 22 (right), 25, 60
Crown copyright, Public Record Office, page 18
Mansell Collection, pages 33 (left), 38 (both photographs), 44 (lower), 67, 70 (top), 73 (lower), 75 (lower), 82, 85
Mary Evans Picture Library, pages 46, 79, 82 (lower)
Phaidon Press Ltd, pages 2, 3, 30
Pierpont Morgan Library, page 31, from their ms 638 folio 23v
Radio Times Hulton Picture Library, pages 15, 33 (right), 42, 47, 64, 66, 70, 73, 76, 87, 88 (top)

The publishers would also like to thank Illustration Research Service for finding some of the pictures of warfare and siege weapons, and the Armourer of the Tower of London for help in locating the illustrations on pages 32 and 34 in early books of military theory.

Line illustrations and plans by Michael Shoebridge.

Castles

The word 'castle' is often used to describe any ancient fortress or large house with battlements. There is, for example, Maiden Castle in Dorset, a huge hill-fort constructed by men of the late Iron Age; there is also Richborough Castle at Sandwich, Kent, one of many forts built by the Romans to defend the coasts against sea-raiders.

In Saxon times, forts known as 'burghs' were built to shelter people from invaders and to provide strongpoints which would hamper an enemy's advance. King Alfred built many burghs to defend his kingdom against the Danes.

But none of these was a castle in the strict sense of the word. A castle was the private fortress of a lord, that is, the king or a noble, and it served as his home and as the defence of his lands. Often, it was a base from which he made attacks upon his neighbours.

Portchester Castle. The stone tower was built at one corner of a Roman fort

The first Norman castles

The siege of the Castle of Dinan in Normandy shown in the Bayeux Tapestry

Private fortresses were introduced into England not long before the Norman Conquest. In the middle of the eleventh century King Edward the Confessor invited some Normans to come from France to help him defend the Welsh border. One of these knights, Richard Fitzcrob, built a fortress known as Richard's Castle, not far from Ludlow in Shropshire. This type of fortress had not been seen before in England.

In France, however, and especially in Normandy, where the nobles were constantly at war with one another, private fortresses were already numerous. From boyhood, Duke William of Normandy had to fight hard to subdue his rebellious knights and he came to know a great deal about the military use of castles. Thus, as soon as he landed on the south coast of England in 1066, he had a castle of earth and timber erected at Hastings. After the battle, he marched to Dover where he strengthened and probably enlarged a castle built a short time before by King Harold, King Edward's successor. He could then advance towards London, knowing that he had a strong-point in the rear to which he could retreat if he needed to escape by sea.

As it happened, there was no retreat. At Berkhamsted, the English surrendered and Duke William became king of England. Immediately, he set about securing the kingdom by building large numbers of castles, probably at least a hundred during his reign.

William the Conqueror's castles

What were these castles like and how did William manage to build so many in so short a time?

Motte and palisade

The answer is that William made a bargain with his followers whereby, in return for the lordship of their estates, they should govern them in his name and carry out certain duties, such as serving him in war. In order to rule a district, the Norman lord was given permission to erect a stronghold and he naturally did this in the way that was familiar to him in Normandy.

Having chosen a suitable site, the new lord ordered the local inhabitants to raise a huge mound of earth by digging a wide circular ditch and throwing the earth into the middle. This mound, called a *motte*, was flattened on the top and here, at the summit, a strong fence or *palisade* was erected. Inside the fence, a wooden tower was put up to serve as the lord's dwelling house and as the last point of defence. Even if stone was available, it was not used, because the mound would not have taken the weight of a stone tower until the earth had settled for several years.

Building the first castle at Hastings. Workmen are making the motte

Beyond the mound was a good-sized yard or 'base-court', called the *bailey*, which was surrounded by another ditch joined to the ditch round the motte. The earth was thrown inwards to make a bank or rampart which was topped by a wooden palisade.

The purpose of the bailey was to provide outer defences for the tower on the mound, as well as a space for stables, barns and store-rooms. There was usually a chapel and a kitchen as well, and in the early period of castle-building, all these buildings were made of wood or of wattle-and-daub, that is, woven sticks smeared with clay.

Thus, the first castles were no more than wooden towers set on top of earth mounds surrounded by ditches and palisades.

Motte-and-bailey

Anyone approaching one of these castles could enter it only by crossing a bridge over the outer ditch and going through a gate in the palisade. He was now in the bailey, but in order to reach the tower, he had to cross a second bridge and climb the path up the mound to the gateway in the upper palisade.

Berkhamsted Castle

Finally, he was confronted by the tower itself. Its basement was a store-room with no door at ground level; above was the living-room or hall, reached by a flight of steps, and above this was the pointed roof. The tower was built of stout timbers and painted in bright colours.

Plan of a typical house of the time

This, the early type of Norman castle, is known as *motte-and-bailey*. Large numbers were built all over Britain, and some of them were altered and enlarged in later years when stone walls and towers were erected. Many others were abandoned after their usefulness had come to an end, though the motte itself may still survive as a grassy mound. There is a huge one at Thetford in Norfolk, where, in addition to the motte, you can still see ditches and ramparts.

At Berkhamsted, the outlines of the Conqueror's motte-and-bailey castle can be clearly seen, now that much of the later stonework has fallen into ruins. Here, as in most cases, the bailey stretched away from the motte, so that, in plan, the whole castle looked like a roughly drawn figure 8, with motte at the top and the lower and bigger part of the 8 forming the bailey. However, the shape varied a good deal, and sometimes there were two baileys, also called *wards*.

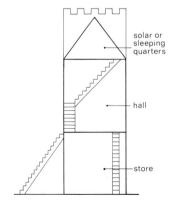

The same rooms in a tower house

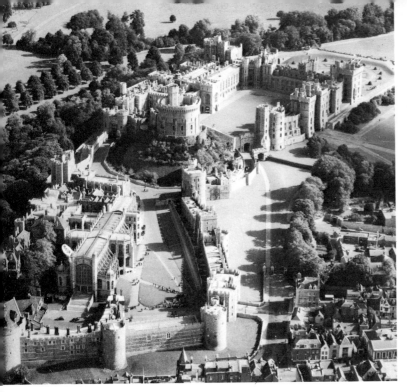

Windsor Castle. The motte and two baileys are clearly visible, though all the buildings were added later

Windsor Castle, begun four years after the Battle of Hastings, had two wards, one on either side of the motte, which was erected on a chalk hill dominating the low-lying country. Though many buildings and royal apartments have been added, this plan is still clear. There was a double bailey at Castle Urquhart, Inverness-shire, and a castle with two baileys was erected at Builth in Brecknockshire, though there is little to be seen there now, except the mound and ditches. At Skenfrith, Monmouthshire, the Normans placed the motte in one corner of a rectangular bailey.

Motte in corner of enclosure — Skenfrith

Two mottes in one bailey — Lincoln

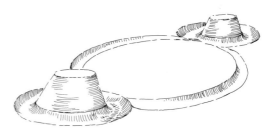

Very rarely, two mottes were raised, as at Lewes in Sussex, and also at Lincoln, where they are very close together, possibly because the earlier motte was found to be unsafe or too small.

Two mottes and one bailey — Lewes

Wherever possible, the castle was built close to a river or stream which could add to the defences and supply water to the ditches. Where there was no stream, a dry moat was constructed. The builders had to make sure that there was a supply of drinking water and we usually find a well in the basement of the tower or in the inner bailey, though nowadays it is often dry. This may be because it has become choked with rubbish or because the water-level has fallen, but in days when it was essential to the defenders the well was carefully tended. Sometimes, rainwater from the roofs was made to flow into a cistern. This gave an additional supply of water.

In places, the well-shaft had to be dug to a great depth. At Carisbrooke Castle on the Isle of Wight, the well is 160 feet deep, while at Dover, the shaft goes down for 350 feet.

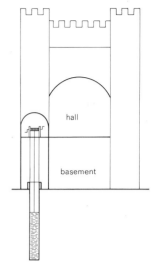

When the well was in the basement of the Great Tower, a shaft was sometimes cut in the thickness of the stone walls so that water could be drawn up to the higher floors. We may find traces of lead pipes which carried water from a tank to various parts of the castle

At Carisbrooke a donkey turns the windlass

What were castles for?

What was the purpose of the motte-and-bailey castles which William the Conqueror and his successors erected all over the country?

The Norman army which came to England in 1066 was not a large one; it may have amounted to 12,000 men, though some historians believe that it was barely half that size. At all events, William had only a small force with which to subdue a nation of perhaps one and a half to two million people.

Norman knights riding out of their castle

Although stunned by the loss of their king and nearly all the best of their fighting men at Hastings, the English were still capable of raising fresh armies. Indeed, some of their forces were on the road to Hastings when the battle took place. All they needed was a leader and it was therefore essential for William to act quickly.

His castles, erected with great speed and efficiency, convinced the English that resistance was hopeless. Around the capital, outside towns, at cross-roads and on natural strong-points, they saw the strange fortresses being constructed and, almost before they realised what had happened, wooden towers dominated the countryside, with guards perpetually on watch for signs of rebellion. By day, grim-faced Norman knights, better-armed and mounted than the English, rode out of the stockade to impose the Conqueror's orders upon a defeated people and, at night, they withdrew to the safety of the fortress.

In case of attack, the castle was a strong place of refuge until help arrived. When serious risings took place in the west and the north, William was able to march against the rebels knowing that his network of castles held the south in check. As he advanced, he built more castles, as you can see in the map.

Important places and old
kingdoms in the time of
William the Conqueror

SCOTLAND

Northumbria

- BERWICK
- BAMBURGH
- ALNWICK
- NEWCASTLE
- DURHAM
- BROUGH
- YORK

Gwynedd

- RHUDDLAN
- CHESTER
- LINCOLN
- NOTTINGHAM
- STAFFORD
- NORWICH

Mercia

The Marches

Powys

- LUDLOW
- KENILWORTH
- WARWICK
- HUNTINGDON
- NORTHAMPTON
- ELY
- FRAMLINGHAM
- CAMBRIDGE
- BURY ST EDMUNDS
- RADNOR

Deheubarth

- BRECON
- ST DAVIDS
- HEREFORD
- MONMOUTH
- GLOUCESTER
- OXFORD
- PEMBROKE
- BERKHAMSTED
- ST ALBANS
- LONDON
- CAERPHILLY
- CARDIFF
- BRISTOL
- CANTERBURY
- DOVER

Kent

Wessex

- WINCHESTER
- ARUNDEL
- LEWES
- ×Battle
- HASTINGS
- EXETER

━ ·━ ·━ South of this line, England was thoroughly conquered in William I's reign.
To the north and west, the barons were expected to subdue the local
population and carve their own estates.

William built a castle at Warwick and one at Nottingham. These new castles so dismayed the northern earls that they retreated and William entered York without a battle. Here, he raised a castle-mound before retiring south, founding castles at Lincoln, Huntingdon and Cambridge as he went.

At Exeter, he took the highest ground in the city and put a castle there to overawe the inhabitants and, later, when another rising took place in the north, his castle at York held out until he arrived to relieve the garrison.

These Norman castles were more than mere fortresses, for they were also the centres of local government. The baron was the lord of the district and all the inhabitants of his manors looked to him for protection and justice. They were his *tenants*, farming his land in return for service and various payments. In the *Barony Court*, held in the great hall of the castle, the baron dealt with crimes such as letting beasts stray into the wheat, cutting down trees in the forest, brawling, and stealing a neighbour's food. The punishment was nearly always a fine, so the court produced a useful income for the lord.

A motte-and-bailey castle at Pickering, Yorkshire

Who held the castles?

The lord who occupied a castle held it as a gift from the king. But it was not an outright gift; the king could, and often did, take it away from a baron who had offended him or had failed to carry out his duties. As already mentioned, the lord only held his estates in return for service to the king and the system worked as long as the barons obeyed him. Under a weak ruler, they often defied the king's authority and fought against other barons in order to increase their possessions. A baron was able to do this because his tenants were bound to him rather than to the king himself.

For this reason, the king tried to avoid making a baron too strong in one part of the country. Hence, a great noble might have widely scattered estates with several castles. He would occupy one himself when not in attendance upon the king, and in each of the others he would place a commander known as the *castellan* or *constable*.

The king himself possessed a number of royal castles, manned by constables and knights in his pay. In the Conqueror's time, these castles, inside an area bounded by Exeter, York, Lincoln and Norwich, commanded the main roads and towns of southern England. In more distant parts, along the Welsh border and in the north, a lord would hold his land and castle on condition that he kept the district in order.

Clifford's Tower at York. The stone tower was built later, on William's motte of 1068

When times were quiet, the royal castles did not need full garrisons. The constable and a few soldiers and servants were sufficient for each, but the king took care to see that numbers of small manors in the neighbourhood were held on terms called *guard and service*. This meant that when they were needed, the tenants went at once to the castle to serve in the garrison.

In some cases, a tenant might hold his land by *castle-guard*, being bound to provide the garrison for a particular tower of the castle, which would be known by his name—Hugh's Tower, for example. Normally, a man did military service for forty days a year.

Life in an early castle

The great hall of an early castle

There was little comfort or privacy for the lord and his followers and they had no knowledge of any other kind of life. They lived and ate together in the hall of the wooden tower, the food having been cooked in a separate kitchen in the bailey and carried across the bridge into the hall. There would have been no great difficulty about this when meals consisted mainly of meat, bread and ale, with wine for the lord when it could be obtained. Since meat was more often boiled than roasted, the great cauldrons were probably carried straight from the kitchen fire to the hall, though in winter, the food must have been lukewarm and greasy.

The lord himself dined at a table set across the top of the room; this was the *table dormant*, a massive piece of furniture which could not be taken to pieces. His men sat on benches at *trestle-tables* placed longwise down the hall and these tables could be taken down and stacked to make more space. The lord's high-backed chair was almost certainly the only chair in the castle. His wife and the principal guests sat on stools made comfortable with cushions. The only other sign of wealth, apart from his rings, his wife's bracelets and a few silver vessels on the table, was probably a piece of tapestry fastened to the wall behind him.

After dinner and when the songs and stories were over, the men lay down to sleep on cloaks and blankets spread over the rushes on the floor but the lord himself and his lady probably retired to a small room called the *solar* which was partitioned off from the hall. The solar's furniture would consist of a bed, a chest and the baby's cradle. Glass windows were unknown and, although the wooden shutters would be closed at night, the Normans must have lived perpetually in draughts.

However, they were pioneers, living as conquerors in a land whose people hated them or, at best, obeyed their orders with sullen unwillingness. In the early years after the Conquest, the castle-dwellers craved not comfort, but security from attack and from the risk of fire.

A beautiful gold brooch, which the lady of the castle might have owned

The solar

Stone in place of wood

The motte-and-bailey castle made of earth and timber remained the usual type of fortress for many years after the Conqueror's reign. Dozens were erected as the Normans and their English followers pushed into Wales; many were built in Ireland when Richard de Clare, known as 'Strongbow', invaded that country more than one hundred years after the Battle of Hastings, and many others appeared in Scotland during the twelfth and thirteenth centuries when Anglo-Norman lords obtained large estates in the Lowlands and the north-eastern plains.

In England, however, stone made its first appearance at an early date. As soon as the kingdom had been surrendered, William I chose a site for a castle just inside the old Roman walls on the east side of the city of London and here he erected a temporary fortress to overawe the capital. But he was well aware of the danger from fire and he decided to build a great tower of stone in the place of the wooden one.

The White Tower at the Tower of London. At one time it was painted white, as you can see from the cover of this book. Many of the windows have been added since it was first built

A tower of this kind is called a 'keep', though the word was never used by the Normans. They called it simply 'the great tower', or the 'donjon', from which we get our word dungeon. Not until the sixteenth century did the word 'keep' come into use

The Tower of London was not finished in William's life-time, for the work, entrusted to a Norman monk named Gundulf, continued into the reigns of William Rufus and Henry I. The great tower, later called the White Tower when it was whitewashed inside and out during Henry III's reign, was enormously strong, with walls fifteen feet thick at the base and eleven feet thick at the top. Its height was ninety feet to the battlements, and an unusual feature was the addition of four domed turrets at the corners, three of them square and one round.

As far as we know, only one other stone keep was built in England before 1100 A.D. This was at Colchester in Essex where the keep is even larger than the Tower of London, though its two upper storeys are now missing.

An old print showing the curtain wall of Richmond Castle, and the stone keep built a little later

Curtain walls and shell keeps

Stone was used, however, to improve the defences of castles which still retained their wooden towers. At Richmond in Yorkshire, the bailey was surrounded by a stone wall called a *curtain*, erected in about 1075, and eleventh-century curtains were also built at Rochester and at Peveril, Derbyshire.

Ludlow Castle. The gate-
house is the great keep on
the left. In later times a new
gate was made, next to the
old gatehouse

At Ludlow in Shropshire, a Norman baron, Roger de
Lacy, proved himself ahead of the times by enclosing a courtyard with a stone wall and building a huge *gatehouse* to serve as
his fortress-home.

In some places, the wooden palisade round the summit of
the motte was replaced by a circular stone wall. This was a
shell keep. Inside the shell, the old wooden tower was
demolished to make room for buildings of stone. The Round
Tower at Windsor was originally a shell keep and there is a
fine one at Restormel in Cornwall, as well as others at Cardiff,
Lewes, Lincoln, Carisbrooke, and Pickering in Yorkshire.

Restormel Castle in
Cornwall

Stone keeps

During the twelfth century, enormous stone keeps, similar to the two raised by the Conqueror, were erected in many parts of the country. Among the earliest were Rochester, Norwich, Corfe and Sherborne in Dorset, Castle Hedingham in Essex, Pevensey in Sussex, and Portchester in Hampshire (the last two being built inside the walls of Roman forts).

In the second half of the century, the reign of Henry II (1154–89) became the great era of the square keep. Because these huge towers have survived better than almost any other buildings ever raised in Britain, some people think that this was the standard type of medieval castle. It was not. As we shall see, castle design was constantly advancing for the next 300 years at least and the massive square keep went out of fashion in a comparatively short time.

At his accession, Henry II found that a large number of castles had been erected without royal permission. During the reign of his predecessor, Stephen, there had been a civil war in

The great square keep at Rochester, Kent

which some of the barons fought for Stephen and some for Matilda, the mother of Henry II. The barons often changed sides or engaged in private war with their neighbours. As the *Anglo-Saxon Chronicle* records:

> They filled the land with castles. . . . They greatly oppressed the wretched people by making them work at these castles and when the castles were finished, they filled them with devils and evil men. . . .

In short, the castle was no longer a Norman fortress built to hold down a conquered population, but it had become a private stronghold that was the proof of a baron's power and the means of making war whenever he pleased.

Henry II, determined to be master of his kingdom, destroyed a great many of the illegal or *adulterine* castles, which was not a difficult task since most were of the motte-and-bailey type. Others he took into his own hands, occasionally returning a castle to the former owner on payment of a large fine. Then, to strengthen his own position, he built a number of royal castles. He built one, for instance, at Orford in Suffolk, where a baron named Earl Bigod was very powerful. He also took over Kenilworth Castle to balance the great Earl of Warwick's castle at Warwick, only five miles away.

This is the original record that Edward Dalyngrigge, knight, of Bodyham (Bodiam) in Sussex is granted a licence to crenellate his manor house and make it a castle.
It is written in medieval Latin in the Patent Roll of 1385. In the second line you may be able to read the names Dalyngrigge and Bodyham

Proud, headstrong and quarrelsome, the barons were a constant threat to law and order and, often, to the throne itself, so Henry insisted that castles could only be built and occupied with his permission. A baron whom he trusted might receive a *licence to crenellate*, that is, permission to add battlements called *crenellations* to a building.

Crenellations

Henry was also careful to appoint trustworthy constables to look after his own castles. In times of danger and rebellion, it was the constable's duty to bring the garrison up to fighting strength and to see that stocks of weapons and food were taken into the store-rooms.

At other times, the constable governed the district and kept the castle in repair. The cost was met by the Royal Treasury or Exchequer and the wily Henry sent officials called *viewers* to see that the money had been properly spent.

The king himself was forever on the move, touring his domains in England and France, inspecting his castles, giving judgment to his subjects and keeping a wary eye on the barons, many of whom longed for a return to the days of pillage and private warfare.

Seal of Robert Fitzwalter, Constable of Baynard's Castle which stood in the City of London

A square keep

Let us imagine that, as members of the king's company, we are on a visit to one of his castles. For a long time, we see the castle ahead of us, a huge tower of stone, so much mightier than the old-fashioned wooden tower on the mound, and, as we draw near, we find that the old motte-and-bailey plan has been altered. The bailey is still there, a large courtyard, now enclosed by a stone wall, but, after we have passed over the ditch by a drawbridge and through the gatehouse, we see that the Great Tower is standing, not on a mound of earth, but solidly on level ground.

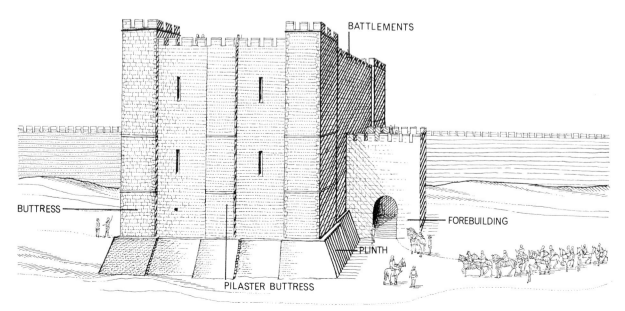

BATTLEMENTS

BUTTRESS

FOREBUILDING

PLINTH

PILASTER BUTTRESS

The foot of a pilaster
buttress

The walls of the Great Tower do not rise sheer, for they are splayed out at the base to form a strong *plinth*. This adds strength to the tower and causes stones and liquids cast down from the battlements to bounce or splash upon attackers.

At each corner, the walls jut out into *buttresses*, which extend beyond the top of the walls to make four turrets. There are similar flat or *pilaster* buttresses running up the face of each wall midway between the corners.

If we look carefully, we see that the walls are not made of blocks of stone but mostly of flints, rubble and stones mixed with mortar to make a mass that has set as hard as rock. Part of the outer surface of the tower, the corners, the arches of windows and doors, as well as the linings of the chief rooms inside are made of squared, carefully hewn stone called *ashlar*. The best stone of all comes from Caen in Normandy.

Plan of a typical great ▶
tower

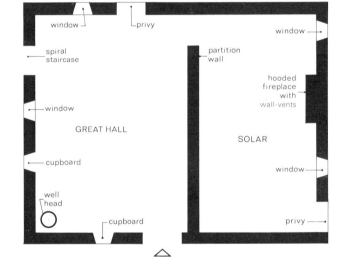

There is no way into the keep at ground level, so we have to ascend a flight of steps, guarded by an outer tower called the *fore-building* or *fore-work*. As we do so, we notice that an attacker would have his left side against the wall and, since he would carry his shield on that side, the right side of his body would be unprotected.

The steps lead us into an entrance room, the *vestibule*, and, in front of the open two-leaved door, we notice that the *portcullis* has been raised to admit us. This is a strong wooden frame, reinforced with iron, which, set in deep grooves, can be raised or lowered by chains inside.

A portcullis

From the vestibule, where the guards are stationed, we enter the *great hall* or *great chamber*, a lofty room which is fairly well lit because the walls have been whitewashed to reflect light from the windows. These windows are small and narrow but each is set in a recess shaped like a funnel and this has the effect of spreading light into the hall. The wooden shutters are open so that the wind sweeps through and we are glad of the fire blazing in a brazier on the stone-flagged floor.

As we look round, we notice on our left a cupboard or *aumbry*, cut in the thickness of the wall, and in the corner stands the *well-head* with its windlass to draw up water for the household. In the outer wall, there is an aumbry for robes and plate, then a deep window recess and, in the far corner, an opening through which we glimpse a spiral staircase. In the far wall opposite us, is another window and an opening leading into a narrow passage at the end of which is a latrine or *garde-robe*. It is also called a *privy*, though in the twentieth century it will be known as a lavatory or toilet. This little room is fitted with a wooden seat and has a channel cut downwards through the wall to the base of the tower.

Meanwhile, we notice that the wall on our right is an immense partition, running right across the keep, and dividing

A room in the keep at Castle Rising. The original entrance was through the fine Norman arch but in Tudor times, as you can see, it was bricked up to make a fireplace

A spiral staircase

A mural gallery

it into two from top to bottom. This adds to the castle's strength and provides another room, called the *solar*, beyond the great hall. This is where the constable goes when he withdraws from the garrison to join his family and to sleep at night. The room is more comfortable than the hall. The walls are plastered and painted in bright colours, and there is a huge fireplace between two window recesses, with a stone canopy to lead the smoke, not up a chimney, but into several vents cut through the wall.

The two principal rooms of the keep—the great chamber and the solar—are covered by a high-pitched wooden roof, hidden from the outside by the main walls. If we return to the spiral staircase whose stone treads are let into a central pillar called the *newel*, we shall find that the stairs wind upwards to the right. This meant that an attacker would find it difficult to wield his sword because of the central pillar. But a defender coming down the stair to meet him would not be hampered in this way. At the top we shall find ourselves in a *mural gallery*. This is a passage cut in the thickness of the walls, with loop-holes on the outer side from which archers can fire down at an enemy. On the inner side of the passage, we can see the roof and its gutters. At the top of the keep, we come out on to the *battlements* which have a *wall-walk* for the defenders.

Retracing our steps, we find that the staircase takes us down past the great hall into the basement or *undercroft*. This is a huge dim space with no door leading into the open air but only narrow slits set high up in the walls to admit some light. The whole area is used as a store-room for provisions and, to save the labour of carrying sacks of flour and sides of bacon up the narrow staircase, a vertical shaft has been cut so that they can be hoisted to the vestibule.

Some other keeps

The keep which we have visited is a simple one, with just one main floor above the basement. It resembles the keep at Portchester, built in about 1130, but Henry II would have considered it too low, small and old-fashioned. Indeed, he had the keep at Portchester raised in height, giving it two floors above the hall to provide extra accommodation for visitors and to make the tower more imposing as a military fortress.

Henry, full of energy and ideas, always travelled with a large retinue of courtiers, officials and servants, and he replaced the wooden sheds in Portchester's inner bailey by new buildings of stone, including royal sleeping chambers, store-rooms and a kitchen.

Portchester Castle as it must have looked at the end of Henry II's reign. You can see where the keep has been raised above the original buttresses

The Upper Chapel at Dover

The keep of Dover Castle
from the air. The fore-
building is nearest to us

Among the many castles built by Henry II, the two most impressive stand at opposite ends of the kingdom, one at Dover and the other at Newcastle-upon-Tyne. Both keeps are tremendous structures, built within ten years of each other by the same master-mason named Maurice, whose fine work earned him an increase in pay. Whereas Newcastle's keep cost over £900 to build, the one at Dover cost over £2000 in the first two years and at least £4000 in all. It was the larger of the two and Henry intended it to be the strongest castle in England.

Both keeps have two floors above the basement, with huge halls and walls of such exceptional thickness that they have many small chambers opening off the main rooms. Maurice supplied each keep with a well room from which water was carried to other rooms through lead pipes. Newcastle has a beautiful chapel and Dover has two, one above the other.

A feature of both castles is the massive *fore-building*, originally with three towers, built to protect the flight of steps leading to the entrance. At Dover, this entrance was at first-floor level but, at Newcastle, for greater security, the way into the keep was high up on the *second* floor.

A basement and two storeys was the most popular arrangement of a square keep but there were plenty of exceptions, Rochester Castle and Castle Hedingham, for example, have three storeys and Norham in Northumberland has four.

Nor was every keep a tall square tower. Some were oblong or multi-sided and a few were greater in breadth than they were high. Castle Rising, in Norfolk, also built in Henry II's reign, is a magnificent example of a squat rectangular keep. It stands in a large bailey surrounded by a huge earth rampart, once topped by a curtain wall, and the keep itself has several unusual features.

More richly decorated and finished than most keeps of the period, it lacks the air of a grim fortress and seems to be, rather, a strong, gracious dwelling house. The entrance door in the fore-building leads to the foot of a splendid straight staircase that takes us up to the great hall, which used to be entered by a most beautiful Norman arch. The arch was bricked up in Tudor times and turned into a fireplace. The windows are unusually large and, alongside the great hall, there runs a gallery leading to several smaller rooms, one of which has a huge circular fireplace. On this floor there is also a chapel and the lord's solar. Below, in the basement which is divided into two parts by a cross-wall, we find the well and ample space for stores and, almost certainly, the castle's main kitchen.

The keep at Castle Rising stands in a large bailey, with an earth rampart. There was once a curtain wall

Such variations between one castle and another built at about the same time reveal the skill and enthusiasm of those who designed them. The king and the barons were constantly taking up new ideas and bringing clever master-masons from abroad to advise them in the planning of new castles and improvements. The French had long experience of castle-building and their master-masons were thought to be the best in the business. As at Castle Rising, the English barons were not concerned solely with defence, for they were beginning to think a little more about comfort and convenience. The castle was a home as well as a fortress.

Orford Castle: a new type of keep

Henry II is said to have taken great delight in the castle which he built at Orford in Suffolk to protect the port of Orford and also to impress Hugh Bigod, a powerful earl, who was himself the holder of four castles in East Anglia.

When it was finished at a cost of £1400, Orford was regarded as a marvel of modern design. Its layout was much more advanced than that of almost any other castle of the time and, indeed, for a good many years to come.

The keep at Orford was neither square nor oblong, but circular, with three rectangular towers jutting out from the drum-like centre. This novel arrangement gave important advantages to the defenders. The inside layout is a triumph of ingenious planning

There were three main floors: (1) the basement; (2) the first floor, containing the lower hall; and (3) the second floor, containing the upper hall. Each floor was reached by a spiral staircase placed in one of the three towers, while the other two towers contained rooms which were important to the comfort of those who lived in the castle. Since these smaller rooms did not have to be so lofty as the halls, two were placed one on top of the other, occupying the height required for a hall.

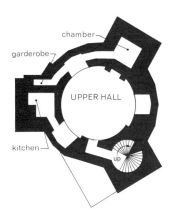

Second floor plan

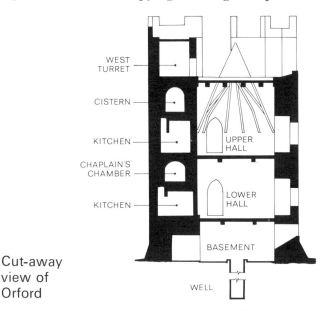

Cut-away view of Orford

Today, we can visit Orford and, since its recent restoration, see this remarkable plan almost exactly as it was 800 years ago.

The way into the keep is up the usual flight of steps to a vestibule from which we enter a splendid circular room, the lower hall, which has a large fireplace with a chimney instead of the old-fashioned wall-vents. The room is well lighted by three windows, each set in a deep recess. Stepping into the first recess, we find a short passage leading to a kitchen which is actually in one of the three towers. Here is a double fire-place, one side of which doubtless contained an oven, and a sink with a drain cut through the outer wall. Another passage leads into a garde-robe or lavatory.

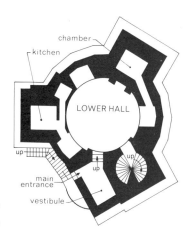

First floor plan

From the opposite window recess in the hall, we enter a chamber which was probably the principal bedroom and, in the third window recess, a short staircase leads to another chamber above the previous bedroom. These two rooms are in the second of the three towers.

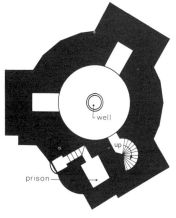

Basement plan

The third tower contains a spiral or newel staircase connecting all the floors. Going up, we find a passage leading to the chapel which is in the upper part of the fore-building, above the vestibule. There is also the chaplain's room and his private garde-robe.

If we continue up the stairs, we come next to the upper hall, another fine circular room in which the king himself probably dined during his visits. As on the floor below, the window recesses lead to several smaller rooms, including a second kitchen, a bed-chamber with a drain at floor-level, perhaps for bath-water, a garde-robe and two large cupboards. A room above the kitchen is thought to have been a water cistern.

The staircase leads finally to the roof, conical in Henry II's time, and to the battlements of the three towers. Even up here, high above the wind-swept marshes, the comfort of the defenders was not forgotten, for, in addition to shelters and store-rooms, there is a large oven in which food must have been cooked and bread baked for the sentinels.

This remarkable keep was designed and started only ninety-nine years after the Battle of Hastings. The inclusion of internal kitchens, private bedrooms and lavatories shows that the castle had made great advances since the days of the wooden tower on the mound.

Conisbrough Castle, Yorkshire, as it was in about 1220

Bothwell Castle, on the River Clyde. The donjon is the biggest of the three round towers

Round keeps

A similar keep was built about ten years later in Yorkshire; this was Conisbrough Castle, a circular tower supported by six buttresses, and there is another at Chilham in Kent. Early in the thirteenth century, a completely circular keep was raised at Pembroke, while at Skenfrith, in Monmouthshire, the Norman motte was used as the base on which a round keep was built in about 1220. This was high enough to permit the garrison to shoot over the surrounding wall.

Not many round keeps were built, though the fashion reached Scotland where the greatest of the round donjons is Bothwell Castle on the River Clyde. Builders had discovered that a circular keep possessed military advantages over the square Norman keep, but after a number had been built, the keep itself went out of fashion. To understand more about the role of castles in war, we must look at the methods of attacking and defending them.

Sieges—attack and defence

The motte-and-bailey castle was perfectly suited to the methods of warfare in the Conqueror's time. Its ditches, palisade and steep-sided motte were designed to repel assaults by mailed knights supported by archers and lesser fighting-men on foot.

The attackers relied upon speed, surprise and determined rushes to force the outer gate or to get over the palisade by means of scaling-ladders. Then, their best hope of destroying the wooden tower was to set it on fire. To combat this danger, defenders often draped the tower with hides which could be drenched with water; similar protection was given to wooden siege-machines introduced later.

But the best answer to the threat of fire was to build a stone keep with *battlements*. Round the top of the walls ran a *wall-walk* for the defenders who were screened by an upper wall called the *parapet*. This consisted of solid sections broken by gaps; the solid portions, called *merlons*, gave shelter to an archer while he re-loaded; then he fired through the gap or *embrasure*. For a time, the tall massive keep seemed impregnable.

Setting fire to the Castle of Dinan

Wall-walk on top of a square keep

It is important to remember that the chief weapon used in castle-warfare was the *cross-bow* and not the long-bow. The cross-bow was so powerful that the string had to be drawn back by a small windlass. To do this, the archer held the bow downwards, often placing his foot in a stirrup to steady it, and cranked a handle. Then he raised the bow to his shoulder and fired it like a modern gun. It fired a short heavy arrow called a *bolt* or *quarrel* with great force and over bigger distances than the English long-bow could achieve. Its range was about 300 yards. It was, however, slower and more cumbersome to use, but this did not matter so much during siege operations as it did in battle. Up on the battlements, the cross-bowman usually had an assistant loading a spare bow in readiness and he needed, above all, accuracy and as great a range as possible in order to pick off the attackers.

During the First Crusade of 1096, the knights of Western Europe found that the methods of attacking and defending castles and fortified towns in the Middle East were much more advanced than any they had known in England and France. With their enthusiasm for everything connected with war, they learned quickly and brought the new ideas home.

First, they improved the methods of attack. A high wall which could not be tackled by scaling-ladders had to be attacked at its base, preferably at its weakest point which, in the square keep, was one of the corners. It was easier to knock out a stone on a corner than one which was set in a straight or curved wall.

Loading an early cross-bow, without a winch

A mangonel being used during the Crusades

A battering-ram, with a metal point

A great tree-trunk, the *ram*, slung by chains from a strong frame, was swung against the corner in the hope that this constant battering would dislodge stones and cause the wall to crumble. Another device was the *bore*, a heavy beam with a sharp iron point which was used rather like a corkscrew to bore a hole in the wall.

Obviously, the men using these *siege engines* had to be protected from arrows and from missiles hurled down from the battlements, so a roofed shelter called the *cat* or *penthouse* was brought up to protect them. There was also the *mantlet*, a movable shield that enabled workmen to approach the walls, while providing cover for archers who were countering the defenders' fire.

More to be feared than the battering-ram was the *mine*. This was a tunnel dug underneath the foundations of either the curtain or the keep. The attackers supported the foundations by wooden props until, when the mine was finished, the props were set on fire. When they had burned away, a section of the wall collapsed.

This was what happened at Rochester in 1215, when King John laid siege to the castle held by supporters of his rebellious

A mantlet

barons. The siege was a hot one, with both sides gaining and losing the advantage. After six weeks, when John had lost many men through accurate shooting and the garrison had eaten their horses and were nearly starving, the king's engineers informed him that a mine under the south-east corner of the keep was complete. To make sure that the wooden props would burn quickly, forty fat pigs were slaughtered to provide boiling fat which was poured over bundles of faggots placed in the mine.

The plan worked. The corner crashed down and the king's soldiers rushed through a gap in the wall. Even so, the defenders held out for some time behind the inner cross-wall until they were forced by hunger to surrender.

A success of this kind had one serious drawback. The victor now possessed a semi-ruined castle which would be difficult to hold if his enemies recovered. In any case, he would be put to the trouble and expense of repairing the keep.

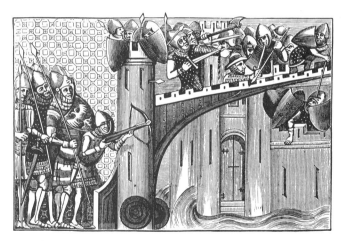

A rolling siege tower used as a bridge. It was made of wood, not stone as the picture seems to show

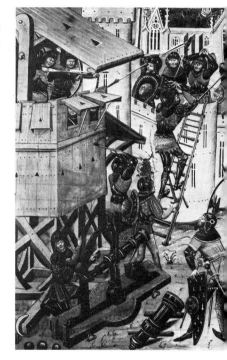

A siege-tower and early guns in use in the fifteenth century

When walls were built so high that it was well-nigh impossible to use scaling-ladders, the attackers would fill in a section of the moat with faggots and rubbish in order to bring up a tall siege-tower called a *belfry*. From a platform at its top, archers would pick off the defenders while a bridge was thrown across to the wall to enable a force to storm the castle.

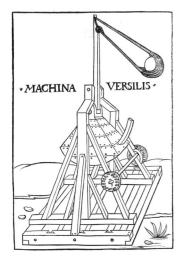

A trebuchet

Various machines were constructed to hurl missiles at the castle. The *ballista* was an outsize cross-bow on a stand; a strong winch drew back the bow-string in order to fire heavy bolts. The *mangonel* hurled big stones from a beam which was pulled backwards between twisted ropes. The ropes acted like powerful elastic when the beam was released. Sometimes, vessels filled with *Greek fire*, a much-dreaded inflammable liquid, were shot by the mangonel over the battlements causing terror and setting fire to wooden buildings in the bailey.

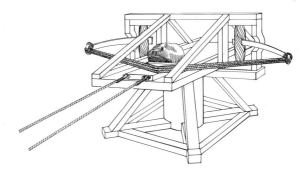

A ballista

In the later Middle Ages, an improvement on the mangonel was the *trebuchet*; its hinged beam had a heavy counter-poise weight at one end that caused the beam to fly upright with great force.

An energetic commander would use every means of attack within his power, carrying on assaults with machines and storming parties, whilst completely surrounding the castle to make sure that no stores or reinforcements reached it from outside.

The reduction of Bedford Castle

Military training, 1280

An instance of the successful use of siege engines occurred at Bedford in 1221. After the death of King John, Hubert de Burgh and many of the barons rallied to the support of John's little son, Henry III. For several years they fought to rid the country of a French army and of the lawless foreigners whom John had befriended. One of the worst of these was Falkes de Breauté who had acquired numerous estates and several castles, including Bedford Castle.

Hubert marched an army to Bedford where he found that the castle's defences consisted of a curtain wall, a keep and an outwork called the *barbican*. This was an additional gateway built to give increased protection to the main entrance. Bedford Castle was well-provisioned and garrisoned and Falkes fully expected the castle to be able to hold out for a year. Hubert began his attack by bringing up two wooden towers from the top of which his archers shot down so many of the defenders of the outwork that the barbican was taken by storm. Next, seven siege engines were brought against the curtain wall until it was breached and all the cattle and horses of the garrison fell into the hands of the besiegers.

Now the keep itself came under attack. Sheltered by a *cat*, Hubert's *sappers*, or mining engineers, dug a mine under the huge walls and, when all was ready, set fire to the wooden props in the tunnel. One corner of the keep subsided and a great hole was torn in the wall. At this, the garrison begged for mercy but Hubert, determined to give a lesson to all such mercenaries, hanged eighty of them, packed the rest off across the English Channel and razed the castle to the ground.

Many castles were protected by sea, moat or river, and might be attacked from ships

This daunting curtain wall, with massive round towers, is at Conway in North Wales

Improved defences

When methods of attack proved to be so completely successful as this, steps had to be taken to make the defences still stronger. Loss of the outer walls was clearly a disaster, since the enemy gained possession of all the stores and cattle kept in the bailey and he could then concentrate all his efforts against the keep. Hence, the curtain walls had to be built higher and thicker, but there were still serious problems in defending them.

It was difficult to dislodge attackers working at the base of a wall, since it was almost impossible to lean out far enough from the battlements to fire accurately downwards. This was equally true when it came to defending a square keep, since each corner had an area of 'dead ground' which was difficult to cover with arrow fire and was the very place the enemy would choose to attack with battering-ram and mine.

To some extent, the keep could be strengthened by a plinth which, as already mentioned, caused missiles and liquids to spray over the enemy, or by making the tower wider and thicker at its base, thus giving it a splayed-out shape known as a *batter*. Solid buttresses could be added to the corners to make the work of the battering-ram more formidable.

A medieval pun — the 'battering ram'

The defenders came to realise that if they built towers jutting out from the walls, they would be able to direct cross-fire at an enemy down below. The archers simply fired sideways and downwards. Moreover, if the towers were round, missiles would tend to glance off and there would be no weak corners for the ram to attack. It is interesting to see at Rochester that when the ruined corner of the keep was rebuilt, a round tower took the place of the older square one.

Attackers reaching the wall-walk were quickly dealt with

The next improvement was to erect towers which were higher than the curtain wall surrounding the bailey. Archers stationed on the tops could deal with any attackers who managed to reach the wall-walk, either by means of scaling-ladders or by a belfry.

Round towers at Goodrich, made very strong at the base

The gatehouse at Cooling, Kent

The Constable's Gate, Dover, a massive fortress in itself

The entrance to the bailey, an obvious point of attack, was given extra defences until, as we shall see, it became the strongest point of the entire castle. Roger de Lacy must have realised this when he built his strong gatehouse at Ludlow in about 1085 (see page 16), but his successor, not realising how to strengthen it, altered it into a keep and made a new entrance alongside.

If the bailey walls and the gateway were made so much stronger, was there any further need of the great keep?

Decline of the great keep

By the thirteenth century, the keep was no longer the principal strongpoint but frequently had become just one tower, still the strongest, in a massive *crenellated* wall, nine or ten feet thick and thirty or forty feet high, surrounding the bailey.

In some cases, the old keep remained the central point of an enlarged castle, so that the Tower of London, for instance, stood in the middle of a ring of walls and lesser towers. The keep at Dover, given an inner curtain wall by Henry II, received an outer wall in 1230–40, and at Pevensey, the keep of 1101 was strengthened in about 1250 by an inner curtain.

Goodrich Castle, Herefordshire, commanding a crossing of the River Wye into Wales, was 'modernized' in about 1300 when the old Norman keep erected more than a century before was enclosed by lofty walls with great circular towers at three of the angles. The fourth corner was, and still is, occupied by the gatehouse which was further defended by an outer gateway called the barbican.

Once the keep was no longer the all-important strongpoint of a castle, its occupants could leave its cramped and often inconvenient living quarters and move into more spacious dwellings in the inner bailey. At Goodrich, for example, the courtyard contained a great hall with private rooms and a chapel, a separate two-storeyed solar, a large kitchen and a long building that was probably used for stores and offices.

The Tower of London. The keep is at the centre of two rings of walls

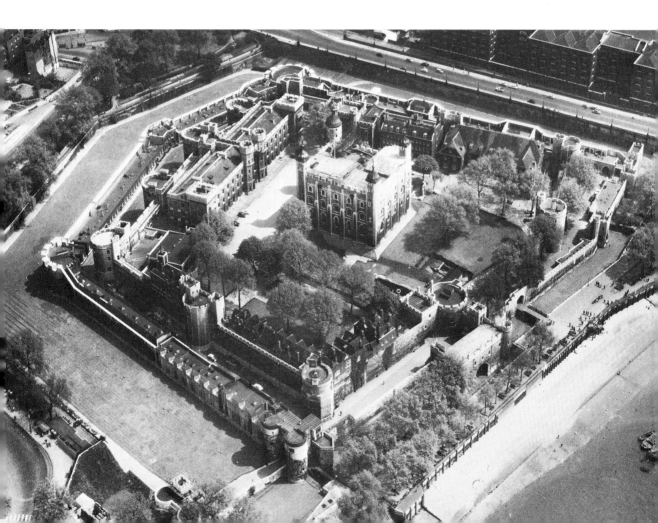

The walled enclosure

These developments meant that the designer of a new castle could omit the keep altogether and this is what happened at Framlingham in Suffolk. The castle was erected by Earl Roger Bigod, after he had obtained permission to rebuild his father's castle demolished by order of Henry II.

In about 1190, Bigod raised a massive wall, roughly oval in shape, to enclose a courtyard containing his residence, and into the wall at intervals he built no fewer than thirteen *projecting towers*, each higher than the wall itself. Possibly, he did not agree with the new-fangled ideas about the superiority of round towers, for his were square. But there was no keep.

The importance of the towers, and of the later round and D-shaped ones, was very great indeed. They divided the curtain wall into short sections which could be covered by cross-fire from two sides and above, and they also protected each other. In addition, they completely commanded the *berm*, the space between the edge of the moat and the foot of   Framlingham

Framlingham as it must have looked. A whole community lived inside a castle like this one

the wall, which the enemy had to possess if he was to launch attacks on the curtain.

If the enemy did succeed in breaching the wall or forcing the gateway, he had not captured the castle, because each tower was a miniature keep in itself. Nor could the attackers storm a tower from below, since, in most cases, there was no way up from the courtyard. The wall-walk went through the upper part of each tower but strong doors could shut off one section of wall from the next. Thus, if the attackers scaled the wall, they were likely to find themselves trapped between two towers.

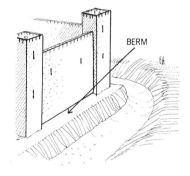

In spite of Framlingham's great strength, the castle was captured by King John's forces in 1215, not long after it had been completed. This might have been due to the presence of sympathisers in the garrison or to the fact that the king's soldiers were foreign mercenaries, tough, ruthless and more familiar with this type of fortress than the local men to whom it was a novelty.

It would be wrong to assume that most castles were held by a single noble family or by the king throughout their existence. This was far from true and we find that castles changed hands with bewildering frequency and the king often exercised his right to confiscate a castle and later to hand it back.

People of the household

Because the castle served as a fortress, a home, the centre of local government and as a hotel for noble visitors, journeying from one part of the country to another, a large staff was needed to run the place.

The lord's most trusted servant was the Steward, usually a knight who acted as general manager of the castle, its land and manors. Next to him in importance was the Marshal who looked after the complicated travelling arrangements of the household when it moved from one castle to another; he had charge of the horses, wagons and fodder supplies, as well as the grooms, harness-makers and wheelwrights.

In a big castle, there were many other officials and servants; during Henry III's reign, Eleanor de Montfort, Countess of Leicester, had sixty persons in her own household. They included several priests—the chaplain, the clerk of the chapel, the almoner who organised alms for the poor, and clerks to write letters—her tailor and his helpers, sewing-women, nurses, a laundress, a barber, an ale-wife, messengers and 'damsels'. Her husband, Earl Simon, who was often away at the wars or on the King's business, had his own company of followers.

The Wardrober took care of the stores in the wardrobe, not only clothes but food and valuable goods such as spices, wax, wine, jewels and silver plate. He kept a careful account of every item which was issued daily to the cook, butler, baker and chaplain

All these people had to be fed, housed and clothed, so stores had to be laid in for them and also for the visitors who arrived with their own retinues of guards and servants. In addition to them and the soldiers of the garrison, there was a maintenance staff of workers—the mason, thatcher, carpenter and smith—whose unending task was to keep the castle in good repair.

Defence of the curtain walls

All kinds of ingenious devices were added to the defences from about the end of the twelfth century. On the battlements, wooden shutters were hung between the merlons. The shutters could be partly raised to protect an archer firing through the embrasure. The merlons were sometimes pierced by a slit so that a defender could see what was happening while he re-loaded or took shelter from a rain of missiles.

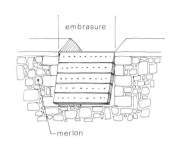

Walls and towers had *arrow-slits* of various types and at different levels; each narrow opening was splayed inwards to give the archer room to fire without making a target of himself.

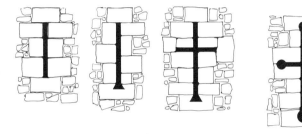

Types of arrow-slit

To deal more effectively with attackers at the base of the wall, a wooden platform was built out from the battlements, with holes in the floor through which stones could be dropped and arrows fired on the enemies below. Not far from the top of the battlements, and on a level with the wall-walk, square holes were cut through the wall; these were called *put-log holes* because beams or *put-logs* were pushed through to support the wooden platforms known as *hoardings*. The hoardings were roofed and the fronts were pierced by arrow-slits for the archers.

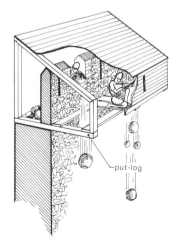

Cut-away drawing showing how stones were dropped from the hoardings

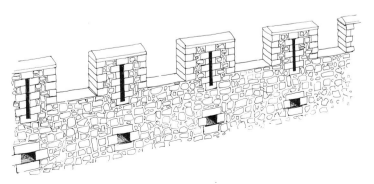

Machicolated parapets at
Raglan Castle

The hoardings were put up during a siege and were stored away in peaceful times. This could be a disadvantage if an attack occurred without warning. The platforms were made of wood, so they could easily be damaged or set on fire. The next step, therefore, was to construct permanent hoardings in stone.

The gaps in the floor were known as *machicolations*, so when stone parapets were built out from the wall with the same kind of gaps for missiles and arrows, they became known as *machicolated parapets*. Good examples can be seen at Raglan Castle, Bodiam, Warwick and Craigmillar in Scotland, but such parapets are not numerous and only occur in the later stages of castle-building.

We sometimes hear of boiling lead and boiling oil being poured down upon attackers but it is very unlikely that these liquids were used. Lead was very valuable and oil was not easy to obtain in large quantities; so the liquid was usually water poured down to overcome attempts to burn the entrance doors. In dire emergency, boiling pitch and quicklime may have been used but arrows and heavy stones would have been almost equally unpleasant.

Meanwhile, the gateway's defences were attended to. Approach to the castle's entrance had long been guarded by a ditch and a drawbridge and both were made more difficult to cross. One kind of drawbridge worked like a see-saw, with a heavy weight on its inner end. When bolts were withdrawn,

Desperate defenders would even throw their furniture at the attackers

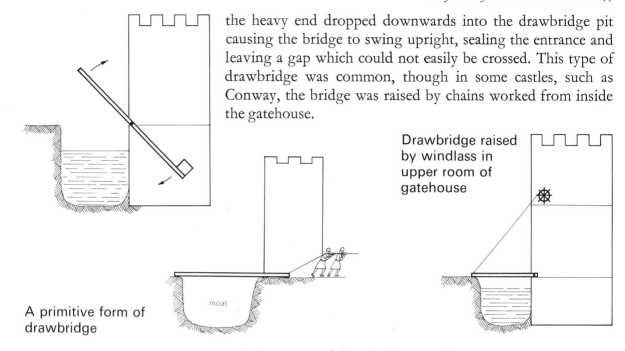

A primitive form of
drawbridge

Drawbridge raised
by windlass in
upper room of
gatehouse

the heavy end dropped downwards into the drawbridge pit causing the bridge to swing upright, sealing the entrance and leaving a gap which could not easily be crossed. This type of drawbridge was common, though in some castles, such as Conway, the bridge was raised by chains worked from inside the gatehouse.

A later type of drawbridge could be worked more quickly, since it consisted of a hinged flap with chains attached to a beam above. The beam had a heavy weight on the inner end and when it was allowed to drop, it simply pulled the flap upright.

Drawbridge raised by beams
above the gate

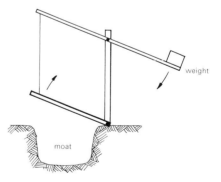

The entrance door itself, heavily studded with iron bolts, came to be placed in a massive *gatehouse*, consisting, as a rule, of two towers flanking a roofed passage-way. Arrow-slits covered the approach which was barred by a portcullis let down from an upper floor.

If by some mischance, the portcullis jammed or the guards failed to let it down, the double-door opening inwards could not be easily forced, because it was secured by a *draw-bar*, a heavy beam that ran in and out of a deep slot cut in the wall at

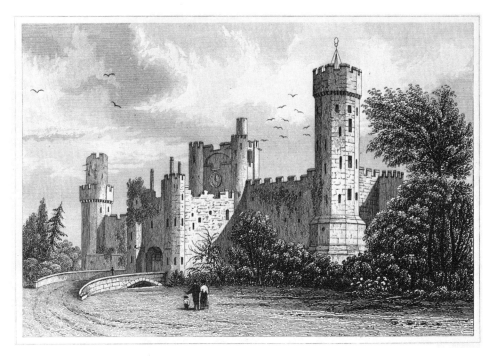

An old print showing the barbican at Warwick Castle

A wagon has been driven into the gateway. The portcullis cannot be lowered

one side. On the other side was a shallow slot into which the beam end fitted. You can see these draw-bar slots, and the grooves for the portcullis, in most castles.

In elaborate gatehouses, intruders who succeeded in passing the first door (perhaps by a trick, such as driving a wagon in, so that the portcullis could not be lowered) would find themselves in a roofed or *vaulted* passage-way, closed at the other end by a second door and portcullis. On either side, they would be assailed from arrow-slits while, from holes in the roof above, known as *murder-holes*, a rain of missiles would descend. In fact, they would almost certainly have been caught in a death-trap, unless, as sometimes happened, the garrison had been taken by surprise or betrayed by traitors.

To make the gatehouse still stronger, an outwork called the barbican was sometimes added, occasionally on the far side of the moat. In effect, it was a lesser gatehouse designed to hold up an enemy before he reached the main defences. It might have been built long after the castle was completed, as at Newcastle, or in later fortresses such as Warwick, it was not an afterthought but an essential part of the defences.

The peak of castle-building in England

The reigns of Henry II, Richard I and John, covering a period of sixty-two years from 1154 to 1216, form the greatest period of castle-building in England. All three monarchs spent the greater part of their lives at war, and since, at that time, castles were as essential in warfare as tanks and aircraft in the twentieth century, all were experts in their construction. The great barons, too, some of them hardly less powerful than the king himself, were still erecting castles to protect their possessions, to keep up with their rivals and to provide themselves with homes suitable for their position as nobles.

The Great Hall of Warwick Castle

Generally speaking, we find that castles were most numerous along the edges of the kingdom. Many were built on or near the east and south coasts where foreign attacks might be expected, and in the 'frontier' areas of the north and west where a state of war lasted for centuries. Barons who held lands in these parts had to protect them from Scottish and Welsh raiders, but in the more peaceful heart of England castles were fewer. They were built there chiefly as baronial homes and to command main routes and important towns.

By the end of Henry III's long reign (1216–72), the building of a completely new castle in England had become a comparatively rare event. There were already more than enough, probably at least 350 in England and Wales, and the cost of building had become too great for anyone except the king and

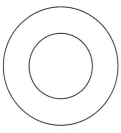

Concentric circles

a few of his wealthiest nobles. Thus, for the most part, building took the form of improvements to older castles where better living quarters were erected in the baileys and a great hall might be added, like the splendid one at Winchester. Stone-built kitchens, bakehouses and granaries took the place of older wooden buildings and, to bring defences up to date, new curtain walls, towers and barbicans made their appearance.

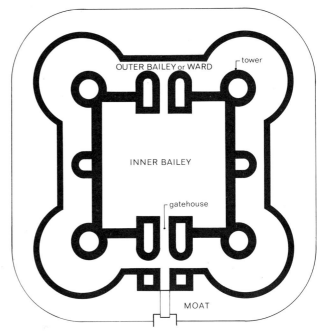

The outer walls of a concentric castle were lower than the inner walls

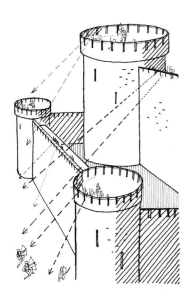

Henry III, no warrior but a great builder, improved many of the royal castles and, by surrounding the Tower of London and the keep at Dover with completely new walls, he introduced an important development in castle design. This was the *concentric* castle, that is, a castle whose defences had a common centre.

The Tower of London became a perfect example of a concentric castle when Henry and his son Edward I added outer walls surrounding the White Tower. This was not an English invention, for the plan probably originated in the Middle East where the crusader Knights of St John erected the immense concentric castle of Krak des Chevaliers in Syria.

The essential point of the design was the surrounding of the inner defences by an outer wall which was lower in height so that defenders could fire over the heads of those manning the outer wall-walk and loop-holes.

As early as 1220, Hubert de Burgh built Skenfrith Castle in Monmouthshire with a keep higher than the surrounding curtain. This layout was perfected in the Edwardian castles of north Wales built some seventy years later, though the keep itself hardly ever re-appeared.

The Edwardian castles

Edward I was a much more warlike and determined character than his father and, while he frowned upon further castle-building by the barons, he himself was soon engaged upon a mighty programme in Wales.

For centuries, the Welsh had fought anyone who menaced their independence and although the Romans and Normans had penetrated the country and had built fortresses to hold the land they managed to acquire, the Welsh had never submitted.

Krak des Chevaliers, Syria

Harlech Castle

Their raids along the *Marches* or borderland proved so troublesome that from William the Conqueror's time, the Marcher barons had been given an almost free hand to construct castles and keep the tribesmen in check.

Nevertheless, by Edward I's accession, the Welsh had become so troublesome that the king decided to put an end to the disorders on the western side of his kingdom. He advanced into North Wales with a large army and defeated Llewelyn ap Griffith (in the Welsh language, Llywelyn ap Gruffydd), the Welsh leader. Then, knowing that the Welsh would rise again if he merely withdrew his forces, he made plans for a permanent conquest. By building castles and fortified towns in which he would place English settlers, he would make it impossible for the Welsh to rebel against his rule, and he also hoped that they would take to town life and peaceful trade.

In order to carry out this plan, Edward had to seal off the mountainous area of Snowdonia, a natural refuge for the rebels. At chosen points, castles would block the valleys and prevent corn reaching the mountains from Anglesey. Each castle had to be on or within easy reach of the coast to allow the garrisons to be supplied by English ships.

In an age when roads were so bad that water transport and pack animals were speedier than wagons, it was a tremendous programme. Vast amounts of supplies and materials had to be collected, and huge numbers of men were engaged to carry out the work.

At Flint 1800 ditchers dug the moats; Conway Castle was built by about 1500 workmen, and at Beaumaris the royal architect commanded a force of 2000 labourers, 400 masons, 200 quarrymen, 30 smiths and carpenters, besides 100 carts and 30 boats.

These workers came from all over the kingdom, attracted by the high wages. They had to be fed, and given some kind of shelter in large camps. They must have worked well, for the huge castles at Conway and Harlech were finished in four and a half to five years. In cost, time and number of workers, each operation was very like the building of a modern atomic power station!

In two respects Edward I was lucky. First North Wales provided nearly all the materials—hard grey rock, various sandstones, limestone, slate and timber in abundance. Finely dressed stone for arrow-loops, windows, door jambs and chimney-pieces was shipped along the coast from Chester, which was also the source of glass for the windows.

Secondly, for architect or *Master of the King's Works*, Edward found a genius in Master James of St George, who had previously served the Count of Savoy, lord of a mountainous district on the borders of France and Switzerland. Master James, the greatest military architect of the age, collected a team of experts to serve under his direction, men such as Richard of Chester, engineer in charge of masons and stone-cutters, Henry of Oxford and Laurence of Canterbury, master carpenters, John Francis, mason, Jules of Châlons, Peter of Boulogne and John of Sherwood.

Conway controls the river mouth

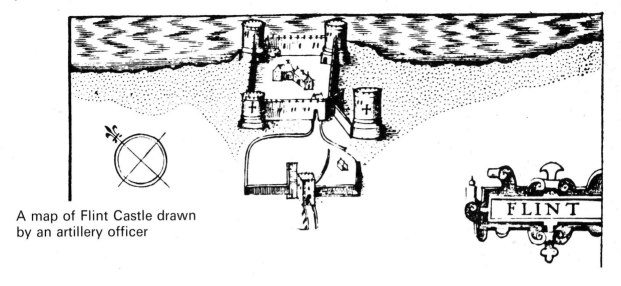

A map of Flint Castle drawn
by an artillery officer

FLINT

Flint and Rhuddlan

To command the route from the supply base at Chester, the first castles were built at Flint and Rhuddlan. Flint's plan was curiously old-fashioned, for it included a keep guarding the entrance to a walled enclosure, and this was probably in imitation of a castle which Edward had admired in southern France when on his way to a crusade some years previously. Master James doubtless knew this castle and made a close copy of it for his royal master but they were soon adopting more up-to-date designs.

The ruins at Rhuddlan still allow us to realise the castle's masterly plan. A square courtyard is enclosed by high walls with identical towers at the north and south corners. At the opposite corners stand two enormous gatehouses which were once equipped with all the latest devices for defence and, on the upper floors, a series of living-rooms and bed-chambers.

Beyond this central structure was a much lower outer wall, ringed by a dry moat on three sides and on the fourth by the river which Edward deepened and straightened in order to allow his ships, forty-tonners, to reach the castle from the sea two miles away. The outer wall was pierced by arrow-slits at two levels, so that, with other archers firing from the top of the inner walls, triple fire could be directed at any point of attack.

A fourteenth-century ship

Harlech: the keep-gatehouse

Rhuddlan was a concentric castle and Master James was soon to design two others at Harlech and Beaumaris. Each had the same essential features: an immense inner wall strengthened by round towers and an outer curtain, which was lower and less powerful.

Harlech, thirty miles north of Aberystwyth, is the most impressive of all the coastal fortresses. Today it stands on a rocky bluff above a stretch of sand-dunes, but in 1290 the sea came right up to the cliff, so that ship-borne stores could be unloaded and taken in through the water-gate.

Harlech's outstanding feature is the gatehouse, so mighty that it can be called a *keep-gatehouse*. Its defences include four great towers, two outward and two inward, with the passage between supplied with sets of doors, two portcullises and numerous murder-holes in the ceiling. Above is a chapel which, rather strangely, includes the mechanism for raising the portcullises. The gatehouse also contains the private rooms of the constable which were fitted with fine hooded fireplaces whose chimney-shafts were cleverly cut to bring four of them together at the top of a single chimney pot.

Rhuddlan, North Wales

The towers and buildings of the inner ward contain an exceptional amount of living-space and this may have been due to the fact that Harlech was the only one of Edward's castles to be built without a town alongside. The country thereabouts was almost uninhabited and the site was difficult to reach by land, so, in addition to the garrison, the castle's inmates may have included workmen and officials who otherwise would have lived in the adjoining town.

We should note that the keep-gatehouse was almost independent of the rest of the castle so that, like the old keeps, it could hold out if the other defences were overrun. More significantly, the constable and his own people were separate from the garrison and this was important in days when the defenders were no longer the lord's tenants but were professional soldiers, serving for pay. Hence, there was the possibility that they might desert to the enemy for higher rewards or might turn against the constable.

The gatehouse at Harlech could hold out when the rest of the castle had been taken

The interior of Conway Castle. Each tower is a separate 'keep'

In fact, there was a mutiny in this very castle when, in 1403, it was besieged by Owen Glendower, or Owain Glyn Dŵr, a Welsh prince who rebelled against English rule. This time, the forty-strong garrison feared that their constable was about to surrender, so they imprisoned him and appointed two leaders in his place. However, sickness and desertion reduced their numbers and, with no help arriving from the English, the survivors, apart from a staunch seven, agreed to surrender.

The castle became Glendower's headquarters, but five years later it was recaptured by an English force numbering 1000 men. Once again, it was starvation and no hope of relief that overcame the garrison.

Conway and Caernarvon

Neither Conway nor Caernarvon was built to a concentric plan because, in each case, Master James had to design a castle for a long narrow site.

At Conway, on a rocky ridge, his plan was simple. The castle, still in splendid condition, is no more than a walled oblong with eight towers, four along each side, and with a cross-wall dividing the outer ward or bailey from the inner

The hall of Conway Castle

ward. At each end of the oblong, a gateway is protected by a barbican and, to reach the main entrance, one has to climb a flight of open steps and cross a drawbridge; the other end is closed by a *postern* or small gate which led to a dock which has now vanished.

The arrangement at Conway was for the constable and the garrison to live in the outer ward. The constable lived in the towers commanding the entrance and the men and various officials in the other towers. The permanent garrison numbered only thirty soldiers and servants, fifteen of them bowmen, together with a chaplain, smith, armourer, carpenter and mason. But the castle had to be able to accommodate a far greater number of persons, in war-time, for instance, or during a royal visit. Hence, there was space for a huge kitchen, a bakehouse and a magnificent great hall whose roof was supported by eight stone arches.

The inner ward contained the royal apartments specially designed by Master James and although the floors have vanished and only traces remain of the beautiful windows facing inwards, we can imagine from the fine fireplaces and window-seats that the castle, still a military fortification, was also a luxurious residence.

This is very evident at Caernarvon, the most splendid of Edward I's castles. Only if he intended it to be the headquarters of the government of Wales and a palace for himself or his son, would the king have built on so vast a scale. This castle is big enough to accommodate a royal household with all its officials and guests, besides the servants and stores which they would have needed.

Like Conway, Caernarvon is joined to its fortified town and consists of a long narrow enclosure whose tremendous walls link a number of taller multi-angular towers and two vast gatehouses. An old-fashioned feature is a great keep, the Eagle Tower, and another, now removed, was the Norman motte in the inner ward.

Caernarvon

A triple arrow-slit

As a military stronghold, the castle was designed to allow a garrison of about a hundred men to travel around the perimeter at speed and to concentrate their fire wherever necessary. Two passages, one above another, run the length of the walls. Archers could fire from the arrow-slits in both passages at the same time as their comrades on the wall-walk above, and so the defenders could deliver triple fire at the enemy, and also move quickly to another point of attack. Some of the arrow-slits were made to allow the archers to work in threes.

These arrangements show us that garrisons had become much more mobile than in the days of the square keep, when the defenders stayed more or less passive in their tower, hoping to wear out the attackers until they lost heart or were driven off by a relieving force.

Beaumaris

When he came to design Beaumaris, the last of Edward's castles in north Wales, Master James must have been delighted. Here was no narrow site, no earlier motte to hamper his plans,

Beaumaris from the air

but a level space on the Isle of Anglesey, looking across at the distant mass of Snowdon. So, beside the waters of the Menai Strait, he designed his masterpiece, a perfect concentric castle.

Beaumaris. Loop-holes in the outer wall permitted archers to fire at the same time as the men above and a passage in the thickness of the curtain wall allowed defenders to move from one tower to another

The aerial photograph shows how a tower or gateway on one side is matched by an identical tower or gateway on the other. This gives the castle a balance or *symmetry* that is equalled only perhaps at Bodiam. Today, the remains of this marvellous castle reveal a square inner ward with four huge round towers at the corners and two D-shaped towers exactly half-way along the eastern and western sides. The other sides are dominated by two immense gatehouses, the southern one never finished on its inner side; being the main entrance, it was provided with a barbican for additional strength.

The outer ward is surrounded by a curtain wall containing twelve small towers and two minor gateways, one walled up because it, too, was never completed. There is a defensive arm guarding the little dock in which a ship could tie up and deliver its cargo.

The sad thing about this splendid castle is that it was never finished. Work went on from 1295 until 1323 and then came to an end, leaving exposed the colossal fireplaces that would have warmed the great hall and, even more impressive, five tremendous window arches for what would have been a magnificent upper hall in the northern gatehouse. Never used as either a fortress or a palace, Master James's masterpiece proved to be a piece of superb extravagance but, in the eight castles of North Wales, he and Edward I had constructed the finest examples of medieval military architecture in Europe.

Denbigh—a private castle

While the king was building the Welsh castles in order to subdue a defeated people and to bring their land under his rule, a limited amount of building by private persons was still going on.

Henry de Lacy, Earl of Lincoln and Salisbury, a baron who had fought against the Welsh, was rewarded with permission to erect a castle and a town at Denbigh in order to keep the district in subjection. His castle was extremely strong, with a curtain wall enclosing a very large ward and the entrance guarded by an unusual gatehouse. This was approached via a barbican, now vanished, and as we cross the drawbridge, we find that the gatehouse consists of *three* towers, for there is a third tower set behind the pair which protect the entrance. This meant that intruders who forced the passage were not yet inside the castle; instead, they found themselves in an

entrance

Simple plan of the gate-house at Denbigh Castle

Denbigh Castle in the eighteenth century

eight-sided hall and they would have to turn right-handed towards an inner entry guarded by another door and portcullis. Caerphilly

At Denbigh, we find an elaborate arrangement of the lavatory channels, five of which were made to run downwards to a cess-pit, flushed by rainwater from a pipe set in the wall.

As at Conway and Caernarvon, Denbigh Castle was joined to the walls of the town built alongside; this was quite a common practice in the Middle Ages when the castle protected the townsfolk and they provided various services and crafts needed by the garrison.

The greatest castle in Britain

Meanwhile, in south Wales, a castle was going up which was even more impressive than any of the king's. Certainly, it is the largest castle in Britain, covering thirty acres in all, nearly twice the size of the Tower of London and its outer walls.

Caerphilly Castle was begun in the previous reign by the mighty Marcher baron, Gilbert de Clare, Earl of Gloucester and Hereford. De Clare, known as 'the Red Earl', was hostile to Henry III and probably did not ask permission to build a

Caerphilly

castle to defend his lands against the Welsh, though he became somewhat friendlier towards Edward I after marrying the king's daughter. Edward, who normally kept the barons in very good order, made no objection to the completion of a castle which exactly suited his own policy.

Though damaged by the Cromwellians in about 1650, Caerphilly is still an astounding fortress. Not content with raising a series of colossal walls and towers on the concentric plan, de Clare turned the site into an island by damming two streams with a wall that also served as a huge barbican. Having surrounded his castle with a lake, he also contrived an inner moat, an outer moat which had to be crossed by a double drawbridge, and a large outwork on the western side which was, in effect, a second island.

With such defences, in addition to the usual portcullises, murder-holes, flanking towers and *bastions* (open round towers or platforms), it seemed impossible that an enemy should even approach Caerphilly, much less capture it. In fact, is was taken in 1327, when the garrison surrendered on favourable terms to the army of Queen Isabella, Edward II's wife, after a siege lasting for several months.

Castle defence

When we think of the problems of defending a castle, there are several points to remember which had little to do with the strength of the walls or with all those ingenious devices that were invented to baffle an attacker.

1. No matter how strong the defences, everything depended upon the spirit of the garrison. If the men were faint-hearted the siege would soon be over.
2. The garrison had to be large enough to man the defences, especially the wall-walk and the hoardings. During Owen Glendower's rising, the Marcher barons were said to have neglected to garrison their castles properly and this enabled Owen to take fortresses that were apparently impregnable.
3. Sufficient stores of food, weapons and missiles had to be laid in to stand a siege lasting for months. Most surrenders were brought about by hunger.
4. An over-large garrison was a disadvantage, consuming stores without adding to the defence.
5. A point of final defence, such as the keep, might be a weakness because it planted in men's minds the thought that the outer defences were sure to be captured. In fact, loss of the outer defences usually so dismayed the garrison that it surrendered without making a final stand in the keep.

A castle which did not surrender would be looted

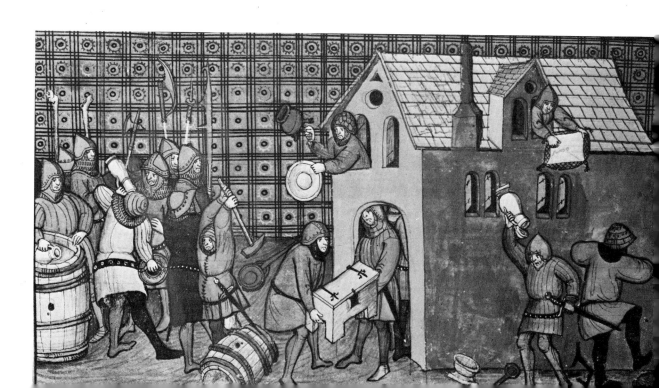

6. Help had to come from outside. This was always the hope of the defenders unless the enemy abandoned the siege through lack of numbers, or moved on to some other objective.

7. It was an advantage if the defenders could strike back at the enemy. When the castle had *two* gatehouses, an armed force could rush out of one gate to drive off the foe who was battering away at the other gate. A small exit for this purpose was called a *sally-port*.

8. Treachery from within was a special danger. Mercenary soldiers usually cared only for pay, and felt little or no loyalty to the lord whom they served.

9. Supply by sea was dangerous, because if sea power was lost the castle became isolated. This happened in Owen Glendower's time, when, aided by a French fleet, he captured most of the Edwardian castles.

Castles in the north

Edinburgh Castle in the eighteenth century

While Edward I doubtless intended to build a series of castles in Scotland as formidable as those at Harlech and Caernarvon, he was never able to do so. The cost of his wars and of the programme in Wales had put him heavily into debt and he was compelled to fall back upon the old practice of building strongholds of timber and earth.

In any case, Scotland already possessed a good many stone castles, mostly erected in the thirteenth century. Bothwell Castle, for instance, with its great round keep, lofty walls and gatehouse, compared well with any English castle. Dirleton, Kildrummy and Caerlaverock castles belong to the same period, all having towers and curtain walls enclosing a court-yard, with one tower, larger than the others, forming the keep.

During his first campaign of 1296, Edward I captured the castles at Dunbar, Roxburgh, Edinburgh, Stirling and Brechin in quick succession and when these and many others fell into his hands, his master-masons usually strengthened or rebuilt them.

Where a new stronghold was needed, earth and timber were used, as for the Peel of Linlithgow, on which 80 ditchers and 107 carpenters were at work in 1301.

The word *peel* comes from the Latin word for a wooden stake used to build the palisade and, as years went by and wooden towers and walls were replaced by stone ones, a peel came to mean the tower itself. This became the characteristic strongpoint in Scotland and the Border country. A peel was usually smaller and less elaborate than a Norman keep.

Edward I died without completing the conquest of Scotland and in his son's reign, Robert the Bruce, the great Scottish leader, regained his country's independence. In 1314 he won a crushing victory at Bannockburn but this battle would not have put an end to the struggle if he had not already taken all the English-garrisoned castles. In one year, his brother

Lochleven Castle, a peel and curtain wall (or 'barmkin') on an island

Yett, and slit for drawbridge mechanism

Warkworth Castle, Northumberland

Edward Bruce captured no fewer than thirteen castles in Galloway alone; most of these were probably wooden peels but the great stone castles were also taken by direct assault or by starvation.

Bruce made a most thorough job of destroying the castles, but the cost of winning independence was a high one. He was followed by a line of weak rulers. After Edward III had made a fresh attempt to conquer the country, Scotland fell into disorder. Violent nobles made war upon their neighbours, feuds lasted for generations and the Highlanders raided the lowland farms.

In this situation, a landowner, even one of the many poor lairds, as Scottish lords were called, was compelled to build a peel, that is, a stone *tower-house*, to protect his lands and provide shelter for his people. Thus, all over the northern shires, on both sides of the English–Scottish Border, we find many tower-houses, ranging in size from the simple peel to strong keep-fortresses, such as Lochleven Castle, Kinross-shire, and Warkworth Castle in Northumberland.

Like the Norman keep, the tower-house could be entered only by a ladder to the first floor. From there, a stair led to an upper room or perhaps two rooms one on top of the other and thence to the crenellated parapet of the roof. This was normally the place from which the defence was conducted. The rooms were frequently roofed or *vaulted* with stone to remove danger of fire, and behind each wooden door stood an iron gate called a *yett*. Iron gratings, often shaped like a cage, protected the windows.

Scottish castles

Because disorderly conditions lasted longer in Scotland than in England, more castles were built there and castle-building went on for nearly two centuries longer, until the sixteenth and seventeenth centuries. Most, though not all, were smaller than their English counterparts, many of them being little more than fortified houses.

A castle was always a home and the Scottish tower-house was very inconvenient to live in, with its rooms placed one on top of another. So its owner sometimes had small private rooms cut out of the thickness of the walls. His next step was to add a wing to one side of the tower, making an L-shaped building. This allowed him to bring the entrance down to ground level, since the door was protected by both arms of the L.

Craigmillar Castle, near Edinburgh, is a fine example of a fourteenth-century L-shaped tower which was later surrounded by a curtain wall with machicolated towers.

The stone wall enclosing the tower-house and its courtyard was known in Scotland as the *barmkin*. It was built on a smaller scale than the thirteenth-century curtain but, within the barmkin's shelter, there was the usual arrangement of stables, barns, kitchen, and often a hall.

Merchiston Tower in the eighteenth century, an L-shaped tower house

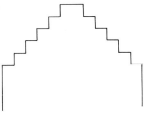

Crow-stepped gables

Scottish nobles had to face the same problems as the English barons when they hired professional soldiers, who could prove to be both rowdy and treacherous. Thus, we find the great gatehouse making its appearance as at Tantallon Castle, East Lothian, and Doune Castle, Perthshire, where the lord had his separate quarters, with the entrance under his own control.

However, apart from such great fortresses as Tantallon, most of the later Scottish castles were built on the tower-house plan with all kinds of variations and attractive features. Sometimes, the staircase was built in the new wing as far as the first floor; above this, the stairs were placed in a turret to provide more space in the rooms. These upper turrets often have pointed caps and, inside the battlements, the roof rises steeply into what was once the familiar shape of a pack-saddle between gables built in steps. So these features are described as a *pack-saddled* roof and *crow-stepped* gables.

Huntly Castle is ornamented in the sixteenth-century style

The finest of all the tower-houses is Borthwick Castle in Midlothian, an immense fifteenth-century stone building with machicolated parapets and high pitched roofs; here, the L has an additional arm, so that the castle is shaped like the letter E with the middle bar missing.

Z-plan castles

During the sixteenth century, when muskets were coming into common use, the Scots designed the Z-plan castle. This was a rectangle with two towers at diagonally opposite corners. This enabled the defenders, firing from *gunloops*, to cover approach from any side, and it would have been just as effective if they had been using cross-bows. The towers were usually round but at the picturesque castle at Claypotts, near Dundee, they are topped by overhanging rectangular 'caps'.

With the arrival of guns, defence tended to come down from the roof battlements to a much lower level and, at Noltland Castle on Westray in the Orkneys, the walls are pierced with many gunloops.

Tantallon Castle

Claypotts Castle. You can just see the gunloops at the foot of the walls

Glamis Castle

Scottish Baronial style

Castles continued to be built in Scotland until well into the sixteenth and seventeenth centuries, when the royal palaces at Edinburgh Castle, Holyroodhouse, Stirling and Linlithgow took their present form.

By this time, war with England had ceased and much Church property had come into the hands of the lairds who used their new wealth to raise castle-mansions for themselves. Built in what is called the *Scottish Baronial* style, castles such as Glamis, Craigievar and Castle Fraser show traces of French influence without losing their Scottish characteristics. Much-ornamented with pointed turrets, intricate gables and over-hanging 'caps', they were picturesque residences rather than military fortresses.

Later castles in England

By Edward I's time the design of castles had become well-nigh perfect, and there was little to be done except to add to the comfort of the domestic buildings.

This does not mean that the castle ceased to play a major role in warfare during the next 200 years. The great baronial families fought among themselves whenever the king was unable to control them, or when their energies were not taken up by a foreign war. The reigns of Edward II, Richard II, Henry IV and Henry VI saw much disorder and bloodthirsty rivalry, made all the worse, at the end of the Hundred Years' War (1453), by the return of mercenary soldiers ready to serve any lord and to do his bidding for pay and plunder.

In such times, the castles provided refuge for the van-quished and protection for many a town and neighbourhood; often, they were the bases from which one side launched an attack upon the other, or they served as stumbling blocks in the path of a victor. No commander dared to advance while the enemy's castles remained intact and so, in the fourteenth and fifteenth centuries, during periods of civil war and disorder there was something of a revival in castle-building.

An early gun. The new weapon made a revolution in warfare

These later castles included most of the features of the Edwardian fortresses, but they tended to be simpler in plan and smaller in size. The prime need was a stronghold in which a fairly small number of professional soldiers could move rapidly from one point to another during a siege; in addition, the domestic buildings had to be grouped inside the walls, with separate quarters for the garrison and for the lord.

Bodiam Castle

All these requirements are to be found in Bodiam Castle, Sussex, built in 1385 by Sir Edward Dalyngrigge when he received Richard II's permission to crenellate his manor-house as a defence against the French who were making raids upon the English coast.

In its straightforward simplicity and wonderful state of preservation since restoration in the 1920s, Bodiam is perhaps the most attractive castle in England. Standing in the centre of a small lake, it has to be entered by a bridge, nowadays direct, but formerly at right angles to the defences so that an enemy's undefended side was exposed. The castle itself is

Bodiam. On page 18 you can see the original licence to crenellate

square, a courtyard enclosed by strong walls with four round towers at the corners and a square tower half-way along each of two sides, and machicolated towers at front and rear. As the plan shows, two sets of domestic apartments, now ruined, were neatly arranged round the central courtyard.

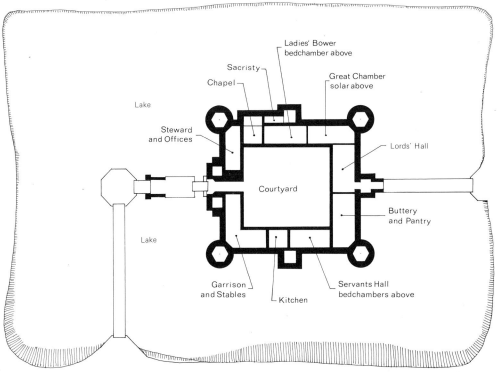

Ladies' Bower
bedchamber above

Sacristy

Chapel

Great Chamber
solar above

Lake

Steward
and Offices

Lords' Hall

Courtyard

Buttery
and Pantry

Lake

Garrison
and Stables

Kitchen

Servants Hall
bedchambers above

Plan of Bodiam as it
originally was

An important detail of Bodiam's defences was the inclusion of *gunports* in the gatehouses. Firearms had been used at the Battle of Crécy in 1346, and by the 1380s they were beginning to influence the defence of castles.

Thus, although the development of firearms was slow and they tended to be more dangerous to the gunners than to the enemy, Bodiam's architect felt that he ought to provide for a few *culverins* or small cannons. By the fifteenth century, gunports became an essential feature, often being cut below the arrow-slits. Sometimes the slit itself was enlarged at the bottom so that it resembled a key-hole upside-down.

Gunpowder brought the military usefulness of castles to an end—but it took a long time to do so, about 300 years. The early cannons, called *bombards*, were difficult to manufacture, dangerous to use and awkward to transport and set up for a siege.

So, for many years, the castle could withstand their cannon-balls with no more difficulty than it had defied the heavier missiles thrown by mangonels.

However, when battering cannon became larger and more reliable, with ranges of a mile and more, there could be little or no answer from the castle. Its walls gave protection from musket fire and its garrison could deal more effectively than ever with direct assaults. But once a battery of heavy guns was set up, the defenders could only surrender or die manfully amid the ruins.

The last private fortresses

When Bodiam was built, the development of heavy guns lay far in the future. Castles were still being erected and strengthened for another hundred years. At Warwick, for instance, the Earl repaired the damage done in earlier baronial wars and added two great towers, a gatehouse and one of the finest barbicans in England.

Brick began to be used instead of stone and Hurstmonceux, erected like Bodiam to repel the French, is an impressive castle with seventeen towers, machicolated parapets, arrow-slits and gunports. Tattershall Castle in Lincolnshire is another brick-built castle and so was Caister, near Great Yarmouth, which is mentioned so often in the Paston Letters, written by a Norfolk family in the fifteenth century.

Tattershall

Hurstmonceux

Leeds Castle, Kent

Nevertheless, the effectiveness of brick walls compared with those massive piles of stone and cemented rubble, remains doubtful. We can only suppose that bricks were used because they made building cheaper and quicker, especially in areas that lacked good building stone.

Stone was used, however, for the splendid tower at Raglan in Monmouthshire which was raised in about 1430–45 on the core of an old motte, and, during the Wars of the Roses, Lord Hastings built, at Ashby-de-la-Zouch, a castle whose strongest feature was a great tower of hewn sandstone. But Lord Hastings was almost the last of the private builders of castles, and he was executed in 1483.

Less than forty years later, the last of the overmighty barons paid the penalty for his presumption when Edward Stafford, 3rd Duke of Buckingham, having erected a great castle at Thornbury in Gloucestershire, had his head struck off by order of Henry VIII.

This punishment put an end to the building of castles by private persons and this includes fortified manor-houses which have often been given that name, such as Stokesay Castle, Shropshire and Leeds Castle in Kent. Wealthy men would continue to erect mansions with battlements and turrets until well into the nineteenth century when Balmoral Castle, for instance, was built for Queen Victoria and Prince Albert, but

these were make-believe castles with no military value whatever. Most people are moved by the grandeur of a mighty gatehouse, and the romantic appeal of castles has never been lost, so that we can easily find examples of country houses, town halls, hotels and even bungalows built like imitation castles!

Stokesay Castle was a fortified manor house. The gatehouse is sixteenth century

Balmoral in 1866

Henry VIII's castles

Deal, the biggest of the three castles, had a garrison of between thirteen and twenty-one

After he had quarrelled with the Pope and made himself head of the Church of England, Henry VIII had good reason to fear an invasion of the kingdom. This could have come from France, from the Low Countries or across the Border from Scotland, and so, from about 1540, he set about building a chain of castles and forts which stretched along the coasts from Hull to Milford Haven. The biggest and most important were the 'Three Castles which keep the Downs', that anchorage between the Kent coast and the Goodwin Sands.

These were at Sandown, Deal and Walmer. Sandown has been destroyed by the sea but Deal and Walmer Castles remain in such excellent condition that we can study their curious layout, and see the way in which the designer used old and new ideas to meet a special situation.

They represent the final stage in castle design which began some 500 years earlier with a mound of earth and a wooden tower. Yet, strictly speaking, they were not castles at all, since none was the fortress home of a lord. They were forts, built as part of a national system of defence against invasion. However, since Henry VIII's forts at Deal and Walmer always had some permanent living quarters and since they have been called 'castles' since the day they were completed, we too shall consider them as castles.

Their architect or 'deviser' was probably a German named von Haschenperg. At Deal and Walmer, he used the local limestone called Kentish rag, with hewn stone taken from the recently demolished monasteries, and he also made considerable use of brick.

Each castle is low and squat, shaped like a flower with a double circle of petals. Walmer has four 'petals' and so is called *quatre-foil* in shape, while Deal Castle is *sex-foil* or six-petalled. Some people believe that this curious shape was a deliberate imitation of the Tudor Rose but it was probably no more than an accident; the architect's aim was to design fortresses which would mount and house the greatly improved guns of the time, giving them a good field of fire, mostly out to sea against enemy fleets and along the beaches to cover landings. The rounded shape of the 'petals' was intended to deflect the enemy's cannon-balls.

At the centre of both castles is a round keep containing the garrison's living-quarters, kitchen, bakery and a basement for stores and ammunition. Around the keep at Deal stand six semi-circular bastions, also called *lunettes*, which are immensely thick and have gunports to command the narrow space between this inner curtain and the outer curtain which likewise has six bastions. One of them contains the gatehouse.

From the basement, a passage leads to a narrow corridor running all round the outer bastions at the level of the dry moat which could be raked by fire from no fewer than fifty-three gunports. Vents above the gunport chambers were intended to carry away the smoke and fumes, and there is a postern gate leading into the moat, presumably for use as a sally-port.

Deal Castle now. It was built in only eighteen months

Since, in addition to these gunports and openings for muskets inside the bastions, there are gun-embrasures on top of the keep and on its two sets of six bastions, five tiers of guns could have been brought to bear upon an enemy. The German architect certainly intended to make full use of the weapons that had ousted the cross-bow! This does not mean that either castle ever possessed one gun for each of its dozens of openings for, while we possess few details of the early Tudor guns, except that they were made of brass, we find that in Queen Elizabeth's reign, Walmer was equipped with ten guns of various types. These were listed as: 'one cannon, one culverin, five demi-culverins, one sacre, one minion and one falcon'.

The cannon's bore was eight inches and its extreme range was said to be two miles while the less powerful guns came down in size to the falcon, with its bore of two and three-quarter inches.

The gateway at Deal Castle, showing the murder-holes in the roof

Notwithstanding his novel ideas, von Haschenperg's castles included some traditional features. Each was provided with a moat, drawbridge, a basement well and a gatehouse fitted with portcullis and murder-holes. The gates at Deal Castle, still in position, weigh three tons and are studded with 1100 iron bolts. If the guns failed to do their work, the defenders were still prepared to receive the enemy in the old-fashioned manner! In fact, the French never came in Henry VIII's reign and it was not until the Civil War that the castles saw some hot fighting.

Decline of the castles

By Stuart times, the newly built coastal fortresses were falling into disrepair like most other castles throughout the kingdom. There were some, like Kenilworth, which had been transformed into magnificent residences.

Reasons for this neglect are not difficult to find, since, under the firm rule of Henry VII and Henry VIII, the nobles had been made to disband their companies of armed retainers and, in any case, the numbers and power of the barons had been greatly reduced by the Wars of the Roses. Both the Henries dealt mercilessly with any noble who showed signs of becoming 'over-mighty', and those who survived, together with the new class of wealthy merchants, preferred the comfort of brick-built mansions to the cold damp conditions into which many of the castles had fallen.

Furthermore, as we have seen, the advent of powerful cannon and the increased importance of battles in the field had reduced the military value of castles. It seemed unlikely that in a well-ordered peaceful kingdom they would ever be used again.

Kenilworth as it looked in 1620 — a stately mansion in magnificent grounds

The Civil War

With hardly anyone believing that it would really happen, the Civil War broke out in 1642 between the supporters of Charles I and the forces of Parliament. At once, in all parts of the country, castles were hastily put into fighting trim, many of them having been seized by a mere handful of citizens. In the towns, it was often the local people who overpowered a bewildered captain and held the king's property for Parliament but, generally speaking and especially in Wales, the west country and in the north of England, most of the castles were held by Royalists. Many a manor-house was fortified by its owner who laid in stores and ammunition and armed his tenants to fight for the king.

During the fighting, castles frequently changed hands, but, as the war went on into years, the Royalists' possession of the majority of castles and strongpoints actually contributed to Charles I's defeat. Far too many of his forces were locked up in passive defence of unimportant places when they could have served him better in the field. Once the king's armies had been broken at the battles of Marston Moor and Naseby, the castles were of little use. Their garrisons held out with forlorn courage but Cromwell's guns and his well-trained army could not be kept at bay for long.

Castles such as Old Wardour, made into stately homes, were hurriedly reconverted into fortresses

The siege of Donnington Castle

Donnington Castle in Berkshire provides a good example of the role played by one of the king's strongpoints during the Civil War and of the fate which eventually overwhelmed it.

Donnington was not an ancient castle; it was built at the same time as Bodiam, though smaller and less elaborate. Its defences consisted of a walled enclosure strengthened by six towers and an unusually tall gatehouse, equipped with draw-bridge, portcullis and barbican. As usual, the domestic quarters were inside the curtain wall and on the upper floors of the gatehouse.

The castle stood on high ground commanding the London to Bath road and the route from Northampton to Southampton, and after its owner, John Packer, had refused a loan of money to the king and had joined Parliament's side, Donnington Castle was confiscated and given into the charge of Colonel John Boys. It served as a valuable outpost of the king's headquarters at Oxford, twenty-five miles away, and, in 1643, Colonel Boys set about improving its defences by constructing *earthworks*, that is, mounds and ditches, all round the castle. The burden of maintaining the garrison of about 200 men—note the increased numbers engaged in this struggle —fell upon the local population who found that the colonel behaved better and paid fairer prices for foodstuffs than many other Cavalier officers.

Donnington Castle as it is today

In July 1644, the Parliamentary general, Middleton, arrived before the castle with 3000 horse and dragoons and summoned Colonel Boys to surrender. Boys replied that he had not learned to obey any orders except the king's, and as for Middleton's desire to spare blood, he could do as he pleased but the garrison and its commander were resolved to shed theirs in the course of duty.

Lacking heavy artillery, Middleton tried to take the castle by using scaling-ladders but after he had been repulsed with the loss of 300 men, he marched away westwards. Another Parliamentarian, Colonel Horton, then set up a battery of guns at the foot of a hill some distance away and demolished three of the towers and part of the curtain wall. The garrison would not surrender, and in October, over two months since the

General Waller

siege began, Horton failed to persuade his men to storm the castle. He therefore moved the battery over to the other side and, under cover of its fire, tried to approach by means of trenches. At this, Colonel Boys made a strong sally, beat the enemy back with heavy losses and captured some of their arms. This set-back and the approach of the king's army caused the Parliamentarians to draw off.

A few days later occurred the second Battle of Newbury in which neither side was victorious, though the king marched away to Bath, leaving his crown and much treasure in the care of John Boys whom he had just knighted. Next day, the entire Parliamentary army under Waller surrounded the castle and Boys was informed, first, that not one stone would be left upon another and, second, after he had refused to surrender, that he would be allowed to depart with weapons and ammunition. To this, he merely wondered that they did not understand his first answer!

The Parliamentarians hesitated to attack; instead, they poisoned a well on the north side of the castle and then, overcome by remorse, told the governor what they had done. Boys led forty musketeers out and in face of the enemy actually cleaned out the well and removed the bag of poison; this was apparently a second well, probably dug to supply the increased garrison, since the original well was inside the castle.

In November, King Charles relieved Donnington and recovered his crown and treasure. This gave Boys the chance to make a sally into Newbury and to repair the defences of the battered castle, not by mending its walls, but by constructing more cannon-proof earthworks which he strengthened with timbers and great packs of wool.

By 1645, the war was going against the king, and after Cromwell had stormed Basing House, a great Royalist stronghold nearby, he sent Colonel Dalbier to take Donnington at any cost, though Boys managed to hold out through the winter and to vex the enemy with sallies.

Their case was now hopeless, for the king had clearly lost the war, and relief, always the hope of a besieged garrison, was impossible. At last, Boys asked for safe passes to allow two officers to go to Oxford and obtain the king's orders; this was

The gatehouse in the eighteenth century

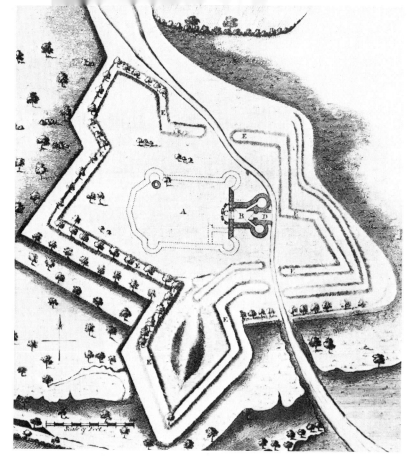

A plan of the earthworks constructed by Sir John Boys. The earthworks were the real defence of the castle and the destruction of the curtain walls was not really important

granted and they returned with a message telling Boys to surrender on the best terms he could obtain.

After a parley, it was agreed that the garrison should march out carrying 'bag and baggage', their muskets charged and primed, 'bullet in mouth' and with drums beating and flags flying. These were the honourable terms granted to a brave enemy, and, on 1 April 1646, just nineteen months after it had first been invested, Donnington Castle surrendered.

This account has been given in some detail because it illustrates methods of defence and attack, but more because it shows that by the seventeenth century the castle itself had ceased to play a dominant role in war. Donnington held out because its valiant commander had constructed earthworks which were far more effective against bombardment than stone walls and towers. If the castle had been totally destroyed, the position would have been much the same; fortunately, the gatehouse survived and still stands upon its commanding hill, and it is good to know that Sir John Boys also survived until the Restoration when Charles II rewarded him with the post of Receiver of Customs at Dover.

Sir John Boys

The 'slighting of castles'

Although Charles I had been defeated and captured, Parliament was fully aware that his supporters would renew the struggle if the opportunity arose. Cromwell was therefore given the task of putting the Royalist castles out of action. Although he knew that a war would be decided by troops in the field, experience had taught him that the castles could have a nuisance value, so he made them useless by blowing up their main fortifications, destroying towers and making holes in the curtain walls.

This process, called *slighting*, was carried out with vengeful thoroughness in some places and less efficiently at others. Corfe Castle in Dorset, for instance, was almost totally destroyed, and Caerphilly, too, was much damaged, though the work of its medieval builders refused to be entirely flattened by gunpowder and one of its towers still leans at an angle, broken but not thrown down. Many other castles suffered in the same way; Kenilworth was slighted by having gaps blown in the outer walls and part of the keep destroyed; Dudley, Goodrich and Bodiam received similar treatment. Rhuddlan was well-nigh demolished, and at Conway the castle had taken such a battering during its last siege, that little more demolition was needed. Fortunately, the orders to slight Caernarvon were not carried out and some castles escaped damage—Windsor and the Tower of London, for instance—because they had been held by Parliament throughout the war. The sad thing about the destruction of so many fine castles is that it occurred when their military value had practically ended.

Corfe Castle

Since Cromwell

No more true castles were erected after the Civil War; the so-called 'gothick' castles of the eighteenth and nineteenth centuries were merely large houses with battlements and turrets added for romantic effect. Most of the real castles fell into ruins, their timbers and stone blocks sold or stolen, their slighted walls used for barns, while the baileys sheltered cattle and sheep.

Fortunately, and before it was too late, there arose an interest in the long-abandoned castles. Between Queen Victoria's reign and the Second World War, a number of wealthy landowners spent large sums on restoration and there were also some local councils which took a pride in an old castle, repaired its walls and turned its grounds into public gardens. In recent years, much of this work has been carried on by the Ministry of Public Building and Works and no one who cares about historic buildings can fail to be grateful to the experts who restore and maintain these ancient monuments.

It is largely due to them that we can visit castles in every part of Britain to understand how they were built and lived in during the six centuries when they dominated the land.

Bodiam in the nineteenth century. People at this time thought that castles were more 'romantic' when in ruins

Craftsman carving a new stone window frame

Visiting castles

As you approach a castle, you will know by now whether you are coming to a simple Norman keep whose outworks and bailey have probably almost vanished, to a walled enclosure guarded by a gatehouse, to a concentric castle or to one of those complex structures like Kenilworth, Linlithgow, the Tower of London or Windsor which have been altered and added to over a long period of time.

No matter how simple or complicated the castle may be, it will help you to enjoy your visit if you have some idea of which way to go and what to look out for. Here are a few suggestions:

Buy a guide-book: these are usually on sale at the entrance. At many of the castles in care of the Ministry of Public Building and Works there are two types: one is the official guide-book printed in rather small type and written in a style that is not easy for the non-expert to follow, and the other is a simplified guide which gives a plan of the castle and a route to follow. So ask if the simplified guide-book is available, and you can buy the bigger book later and study it at your leisure.

Read the guide-book, or as much as you can, before starting to look around. This may seem obvious until you see people stumbling along, peering at a book instead of looking about them.

Remember the changes: the castle has probably undergone many alterations since it was built. You may find that the entrance is a modern one, say, at ground level, when originally it was up a flight of steps to the first floor. Nowadays, the drawbridge is usually fixed but you should look for the pivot-holes in which the old axle turned and for the pit into which one half of the original bridge dropped when it was raised.

At the entrance: if your castle is thirteenth century or later, you should look for the barbican (the defensive outwork) and spend some time examining the gatehouse. Here, as in the entrance to a keep, you will find the grooves of the portcullis and, often, in the room above, a continuation of those grooves and traces of the mechanism that raised the portcullis. The two-leaved door may be modern but you

may see the grooves of the old hinges and the draw-bar hole into which you can thrust your arm. As you pass through the entrance passage, notice how it was commanded from above and from each side by arrow-slits and, if you look up, you may see machicolations and murder-holes.

The defences: as you progress, imagine that you are inspecting the defences and putting some awkward questions to the constable. If an enemy forces the entrance, how will the garrison deal with him? Are the arrow-slits on more than one level? Do they give a good field of fire and allow the defenders to work in twos or threes? Are the wall-walks in good condition and can you see the grooves for the shutters which hung between the merlons? Have put-log holes been made in the outer walls to take the timbers that support the hoardings? Are the towers round or square? Can an enemy who reaches the wall-walk get down into the courtyard? Do the towers project far enough to cover an attack on the entrance or on any point of the curtain?

By the fifteenth century, life in a castle, for the nobles at least, was quite luxurious

Fifteenth–century manor house

Holes for floor joists

The living quarters: remember that a castle was a home as well as a fortress, so ask yourselves where the constable and the garrison lived. There are usually several answers. In older castles, the great hall and the sleeping chambers were usually in the keep but the wooden buildings in the bailey have long since vanished. In later castles, there was almost always a range of domestic chambers on the upper floors of the gatehouse and in some of the towers. You will see large fireplaces and traces of canopy hoods against the walls. Most castles also include ruins of a great hall and various other buildings such as the kitchen, buttery (wine and ale store), granary and chapel which were built against the sheltering walls with their larger windows facing inwards.

Look for the all-important well; this is almost certainly in the basement of the keep or in the courtyard.

If there is no apparent sign of a kitchen, then it was a wooden building that has decayed but you will often find the foundations of a kitchen in the bailey. Large castles often had a separate bakery.

Inside the castle: one of the most difficult things to overcome is the sense of gloom and chilly discomfort as you go from one ruined room to another via a dark staircase and a confusing maze of passages, so you should remember that the whitewash, the gaily painted plaster, the braziers, glowing fires and wall-torches have all disappeared. Most of the floors have vanished, too, because timber decays quickly when attacked by damp and this was one of the greatest problems for medieval builders. Often, we read of castles needing repairs only a few years after they were built and this would have been due to timbers having rotted through damp getting at them from leaky roofs. Towers and buildings inside the walls were roofed with slates or wooden shingles which needed constant attention. Lead, a much better roofing material, was used whenever possible but it was expensive and very heavy.

You will see rectangular holes for the floor-joists of each storey and, in many places, the stone brackets called *corbels* which supported the roof and ceiling trusses. Towers which are now open to the sky usually had conical roofs, though some had a flat fighting-deck.

Windows: what appear to be arrow-slits in many places, as on staircases and in basements, were placed there for ventilation and light. In old castles, you find that outer windows were mere slits with funnel-shaped recesses to admit as much light as possible but, on the inner side, they were larger with double or triple lights. These were usually fitted with glass in the upper part and with wooden shutters below. In a great many castles, the original windows have been enlarged at some later date.

Exterior view of a window. This is not an arrow-slit

Cupboards: you often come across a recess in the thickness of a wall and, if shallow, this might have been a seat; a deeper one was probably a cupboard, while a small chamber without ventilation was doubtless a strong-room for valuables. The small recesses in a chapel wall were *aumbries* for the bible and the communion vessels; the stone basin was the *piscina* for holy water and the little shelf that you sometimes notice cut in a staircase wall held a simple lamp with a wick floating in oil.

Interior view of the same window

Sanitation: this always interests visitors, who are usually surprised to find that the people of the Middle Ages used latrines or 'toilets', as they are called nowadays. These are the *garde-robes*, small rooms or privies, often at the end of a short passage where you find the lavatory seat now covered with a piece of slate or, better, of glass which enables you to see down the shaft leading to the base of the tower. As a rule, all the garde-robes are on the same side of a tower and their shafts often lead into one vent or arched recess which was cleaned out from time to time by servants. Do not fall into the error of believing that the garde-robes were prison-cells! Sometimes in the base of a tower, you find a vaulted chamber which is mistaken for a dungeon whereas, in fact, it was a cess-pit.

Only rarely do you find any provision for washing or bathing in a castle, so we must believe that the servants brought jugs of water to the lord and his lady who washed themselves in basins. Occasionally we find a drain at floor level in one of the principal sleeping chambers.

Dungeons: as already mentioned, the early name for a tower, the *donjon*, changed to 'dungeon', a word that fills us with visions of dismal underground prisons where captives starved to death in chains. This meaning of dungeon probably arose during the lawless days of King Stephen, when, we are told, evil men imprisoned innocent citizens and tortured them. Perhaps the chronicler exaggerated, for there are not nearly so many dungeons as some people imagine. The gloomy basement, entered from above by a ladder or flight of steps, was nearly always a store-room and many a dark chamber was the lord's treasury or wine-store.

However, prisoners *were* kept in castles, sometimes for ransom or at the king's orders, and if you come across a room with its own garde-robe and a draw-bar hole on the outside, you can be fairly certain that this was a prison for important captives. Large castles sometimes have a prison tower in which prisoners were thrust through a trapdoor into a dark basement cell under the floor. In later times, when a castle fell into ruins, one part might have been kept in repair to serve as the local jail. Prisoners of war were housed for years in the castles at Dover and Portchester.

Carvings in the prison of Carlisle Castle

Outside the walls: if you are permitted to walk round the fortifications, there are several features to look out for, for example the plinth or splayed-out base of the keep and towers, the berm or stretch of ground between the wall and the ditch which was an essential point from which to launch direct assaults, the postern-gate which served as the castle's back-door and, sometimes, you will find a well-guarded water-gate to which supplies were delivered by boat.

To sum up, a plan, a guide-book and a pair of sharp eyes are all that are needed to enable you to enjoy your visit to a castle. And remember this, no two castles are alike. They vary in shape, design and methods of construction, and most of them have been altered at various times because the owners, like most householders today, wanted to be secure, comfortable and in the fashion.

Glossary

ashlar blocks of smooth, squared stone
aumbry a wall cupboard
bailey courtyard (ward)
ballista siege engine like a huge bow
barbican outer gateway
bastion open backed projecting tower
batter splayed shape of an outer wall
berm space between wall and moat
belfry tall siege tower
bore heavy pole with iron spike
buttery wine and ale store
buttress thick pillar strengthening a wall or tower
castellan castle commander
cat roofed shelter for besiegers
corbel stone bracket
crenellation battlements
curtain wall surrounding bailey
draw-bar heavy beam drawn across a door
embrasure open gap in battlements (also a window recess)
forebuilding outer building on side of keep, containing entrance staircase, and often a chapel above
garde-robe latrine or privy (it means a 'wardrobe', hence a private room)
gun-loop opening for gun
hoarding wooden gallery built out from wall-top to overhang base of wall to assail attackers
keep donjon or great tower
lunette semi-circular bastion
machicolation opening in floor of hoarding or parapet through which missiles could be dropped
mangonel stone throwing machine
mantlet movable shield for archers
marshal official in charge of transport and war supplies

merlon solid portion of battlement
motte a mound of earth
murder-holes hole in roof of passage, for missiles etc.
newel central pillar of spiral staircase
peel originally a wooden stake; later, a Scottish tower
penthouse roofed shelter (cat)
plinth base of wall sloping outwards
portcullis iron-shod grating, guarding an entrance
postern a side gate
put-log beam pushed through hole at wall-walk level to support hoarding
sally-port side gate for counter-attack
shell keep wall round summit of motte
slighting deliberate destruction of castle defences
solar the lord's private room
steward the lord's chief official
trebuchet giant sling
undercroft basement storeroom
ward courtyard (bailey)
yett iron grating over window or door in Scotland

Index

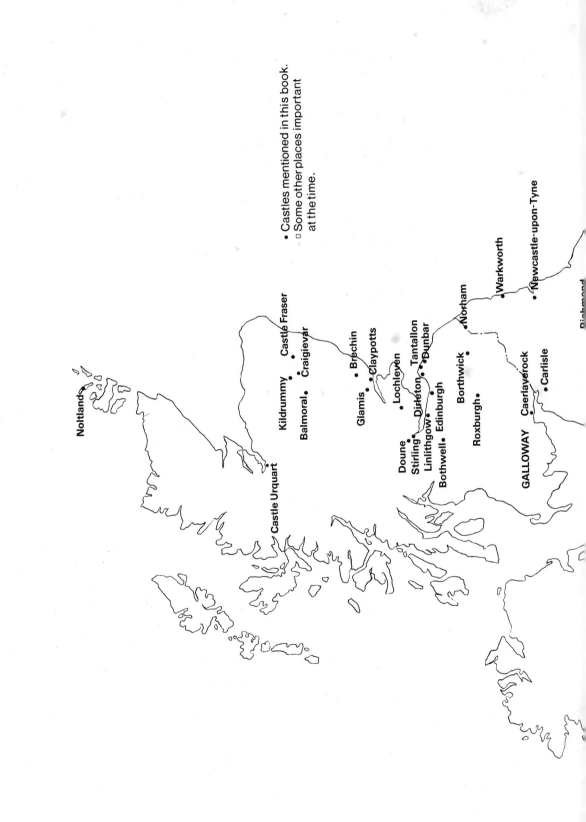

- Castles mentioned in this book.
- Some other places important at the time.

Noltlands

Castle Urquart

Kildrummy
Balmoral
Castle Fraser
Craigievar

Glamis
Brechin
Claypotts

Lochleven
Tantallon
Dunbar

Doune
Stirling
Linlithgow
Dirleton
Edinburgh
Bothwell
Borthwick
Roxburgh

Norham

Warkworth

Newcastle-upon-Tyne

GALLOWAY
Caerlaverock
Carlisle

Richmond